Traditional
jewellery

in Nineteenth-Century Europe

Jane Perry

Traditional jewellery

in Nineteenth-Century Europe

First published by
V&A Publishing, 2013
Victoria and Albert Museum
South Kensington
London SW7 2RL
www.vandapublishing.com

Distributed in North America by
Harry N. Abrams Inc., New York
© The Board of Trustees of the
Victoria and Albert Museum, 2013

The moral right of the author
has been asserted.

ISBN 978 1 85177 729 7

Library of Congress Control Number
2012948898

10 9 8 7 6 5 4 3 2 1
2017 2016 2015 2014 2013

Every effort has been made to seek
permission to reproduce those
images whose copyright does not
reside with the V&A, and we are
grateful to the individuals and
institutions who have assisted in
this task. Any omissions are entirely
unintentional, and the details should
be addressed to V&A Publishing.

Designer: Adam Brown_01.02
Copy-editor: Rachel Malig
Maps: David Hoxley
Index: Hilary Bird

Photography by Dominic Naish
and Jaron James,
V&A Photographic Studio

Printed in Hong Kong

Front jacket illustration:
Woman's bodice
Black felt with 12 silver filigree
buttons. 3.6cm diameter (buttons).
Föhr, North Germany, *c*.1850.
V&A: 971–1872.

These buttons are part of the
traditional jewellery of the women
of Föhr (see Chapter 3), off the
north coast of Germany. Filigree
work, of silver or gold, was one of
the main elements of traditional
jewellery throughout Europe
in the nineteenth century.

Back jacket illustration:
Heart pendant
Gold filigree, length 10.6cm.
Oporto, north Portugal, *c*.1860.
V&A: 1073–1873.

A crowned heart is typical of the
traditional jewellery of northern
Portugal. They are always the
same shape, whether they are
made of sheet gold or filigree.
Filigree is still one of the
specialities of the Oporto region.

V&A Publishing
Supporting the world's leading
museum of art and design,
the Victoria and Albert
Museum, London

Contents

Introduction 6

1 The Nordic Region 20
*From Iceland through Scotland
and Scandinavia to Finland,
the Baltic States and parts
of northwest Russia*

2 The Netherlands 40

3 Central Europe 50
*Including Germany, Austria and
Switzerland, Poland, Hungary,
the Czech Republic and Slovakia*

4 France 68

5 Italy 80

6 Spain and Portugal 96

7 The Eastern Frontier 112
*From Russia to the Balkans
and Greece*

Further information and 134
Acknowledgements
Maps 135
Bibliography 139
Index 142

Introduction

This book is intended to give a brief overview of European traditional jewellery and illustrate some of its great richness and variety. Most of the pieces illustrated come from the Victoria and Albert Museum, which has the earliest and finest collection of this jewellery in the world.

Traditional jewellery is the jewellery worn with traditional, national or regional costume. It reached its peak in Europe in the nineteenth century, when many people still wore these costumes, as had their ancestors for generations. A traditional costume acted as a sign of identity in a landscape in which political boundaries and the links between different areas were often fluid, and could change abruptly due to war and occupation. The jewellery in this book is grouped by area, because that is the best way to classify it, but the areas of diffusion do not correlate precisely with modern political boundaries, and there are no names which can adequately summarize these regions.

In the same way that there are no neutral names for the different cultural zones in which traditional jewellery flourished, there is no commonly accepted word in English for the jewellery itself. Non-European jewellery of this kind is now often referred to as ethnic or tribal jewellery. The V&A called it peasant jewellery in the nineteenth century when it was putting its collection together. It is sometimes known as folk jewellery. All these terms give a misleading and inadequate impression of European traditional jewellery. It was never restricted to the lower classes, and is often very expensive (see plate 105). In several places, mainly in eastern Europe, it was taken up by

1 **Karagouna bride from Karditsa, Thessaly, Greece**
From *The Greek Folk Costume*, A. Hatzimichali (Athens, 1984)

The Karagouna were semi-nomadic herders of Albanian origin. This bride is wearing chains on her hat and breast, two long *kiousteki* chains on her apron, and a series of clasps down her front, including an 'Albanian' clasp at the top (see plate 10).

the court in the nineteenth century, for nationalistic reasons; by the end of the century, when the poorer classes had largely given it up, there was a revival of interest in traditional costume and jewellery among the intelligentsia and folklore specialists in many countries and it became acceptable for fashionable women to wear it. This interest has continued not only among the descendants of the original owners, but also among collectors, students and artists to the present day.

Traditional jewellery differs from fashionable jewellery in several ways. It has been said that it is best defined by place rather than time, and this is a useful concept. What is fashionable in jewellery changes frequently, by definition. In contrast, traditional jewellery is conservative, changing slowly over time, but varying a lot from place to place. It is always much easier to say where a piece of traditional jewellery comes from, than how old it is. Many of the designs are medieval in origin, and some can be traced back even earlier. The use of earrings and amulets in the traditional jewellery of the Mediterranean region is probably Roman in origin. Some designs are no earlier than the eighteenth century, like the large silver shoe buckles worn in northern Europe (see plate 60). But however late its origins, jewellery becomes traditional when the original stops being worn by fashionable people, but the traditional continues in use. Although its original model is usually easily identifiable, traditional jewellery is never a perfect copy. It is more a living descendant, which often assumes unique characteristics over time, making it instantly and unfailingly recognizable.

Another characteristic of traditional jewellery is its tendency to exaggerate. It was intended to proclaim the identity of the wearer, and that required it to be prominent and visible; photographs seldom give an adequate impression of the impact of the actual article. Individual pieces are often much larger than the models on which they are based or fashionable jewellery of the same period. Traditional jewellery is also often worn in greater quantities: if one is good, then more must be better (plate 1).

Traditional jewellery was worn in conjunction with a specific local costume, of which it was an integral part. The association with costume is fundamental, and to some extent jewellery is merely an extension of the costume; it can act as an alternative to other kinds of decoration and there is a tendency for traditional jewellery to be richest in those places where embroidery is scarce, and vice versa. The jewellery is not as specific as the costume, which was usually made in the home by its wearer (or his fiancée or wife, in the case of male costume). Details of costume design or embroidery could therefore identify the origins of the wearer very precisely. In contrast, the jewellery was almost always made by professional silversmiths, and covered a larger area, sometimes an entire region, as in the case of the Balkans. Women often wore fashionable jewellery as well, of course, sometimes even with their costume, but this was recognized as ephemeral and purely decorative, unlike the true costume jewellery.

As part of the costume, traditional jewellery often included

2 **Heart-shaped pendant**
Amber mounted in silver, length 4.4cm. Lorenz Wretman (maker), Landskrona, Skåne, Sweden, 1764–91.
V&A: M.303A–1920

This pendant would have been worn as an amulet as much as a piece of jewellery. Amber was widely believed to have protective powers, and the religious symbols on the back would only have increased its effectiveness.

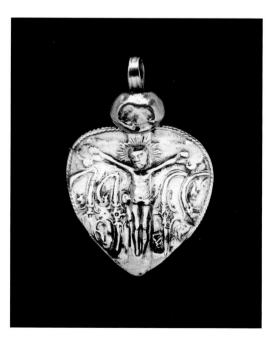

a quite different range of objects than the fashionable jewellery of the nineteenth century. There was a tendency everywhere for mundane elements of costume, such as laces, clasps, hooks and tags, to be elevated to jewellery, as had often been the case in the sixteenth century. Other functional items, which counted as jewellery in some places, included scent containers, purses, and sewing or knitting equipment, and almost every region had some individual item whose use was so specific and obscure that it needs to be explained today (see plate 54). Head ornaments, ranging from hair pins to crowns, were one of the most important elements. There are clear scriptural requirements for a married woman to cover her head, and this was emphasized by additional jewellery almost everywhere. In contrast, some of the most common types of modern jewellery rarely feature at all. There are few brooches, as distinct from the medieval-type ring brooch (see Chapter 1), and those that did make their way into traditional costume are dated no earlier than the nineteenth century. Bracelets are rarely found outside the Balkans.

Traditional jewellery was always functional in origin, although it often became purely decorative. It is useless to try to distinguish between these two aspects. Even those objects which seem entirely ornamental normally had other uses and meanings, which could demonstrate the identity and status of the wearer, or act as an amulet or talisman (plate 2): a finger ring could signify religious affinity or marital status, demonstrate wealth and prosperity, act as a source of value in emergencies, protect against the inevitable dangers of life by the amuletic quality of its design or material (plate 3), or be used as a signet. All were of importance to the original owner. Because of the weight of significance borne by every item of traditional jewellery, its appearance was critical, and small details were repeated for generation after generation until their original identity and meaning had been totally lost – that was simply what they ought to look like.

The importance of getting the details right meant that traditional jewellery was usually made by silversmiths who specialized in making such jewellery, and had often done so for generations. These firms were truly family businesses. The silversmiths tended to marry the sisters and daughters of other silversmiths, and these capable women often maintained their husbands' businesses if widowed, continuing to use their marks where allowed.

The distribution processes of traditional jewellery varied. In northern Europe, silversmiths were usually based close to their clientele, in regional towns and cities. Some of these places developed into specialist centres for traditional jewellery. In Schoonhoven in the Netherlands, the silversmiths made jewellery in the appropriate style for many of the different regions of the country. A similar situation existed in the south German region, where the silver town of Schwäbisch Gmünd produced traditional jewellery and religious souvenirs for a wide area extending to Bohemia, Austria and Switzerland. In Sweden, the silversmiths sold direct from their own workshops, but also rented booths at markets, sometimes at a considerable distance from their home town. In France,

3   **Ring**
Silver-gilt with red and green pastes and deer's teeth (*Hirschgrandln*), diam. 2.7cm. Schwäbisch Gmünd, south Germany, 1800–30. V&A: 170–1872

Hunting trophies of deer's teeth were widely used in traditional jewellery from south Germany. They were believed to impart strength and courage, and promote fertility. That is their purpose in this ring, which would be enhanced by the red and green pastes that stand for love and hope.

4   **Necklace clasp**
     (*Florschnalle*)
     Silver filigree, partly gilded,
     width 10.8cm. Schwäbisch
     Gmünd, south Germany,
     1850–70.
     V&A: 919–1872

The use of filigree in
traditional jewellery was
widespread throughout
Europe. This necklace clasp
is typical of the filigree
made at Schwäbisch
Gmünd, in southern
Germany. *Florschnallen*
were characteristic of
Dachau, in Bavaria, where
they survived until the end
of the nineteenth century.

the silversmiths had little direct contact with the ultimate customer. They sold expensive goods wholesale at the large fairs held annually or biennially at places such as Beaucaire in the south or Guibray in Normandy, or to local jewellers. Lower value jewellery was distributed by itinerant salesmen, called colporteurs, who retailed it at local markets, or carried it on their backs to remote villages. Both middlemen and peddlers were responsible for distributing the Schwäbisch Gmünd goods through the Alpine lands, as well as further afield.

In some places in the Balkans the silversmiths themselves were partly itinerant, and travelled throughout the region, selling and repairing jewellery as they went. This was particularly hazardous in what was a frequently lawless area; Sotirio Bulgari, who specialized in traditional jewellery before founding the modern jewellery house that bears his name, was forced to leave his ancestral home in Epirus and move ultimately to Rome, due to the constant danger of theft or personal harm. On the remote, sparsely populated island of Iceland the silversmiths who made traditional jewellery were mostly part-timers, working as farmers during the summer. Many had undergone long apprenticeships with established silversmiths abroad, mostly in Copenhagen, and there is nothing amateur about the work they produced (see plate 41).

In the same way that people knew exactly what traditional jewellery should look like, most cultures expected it to be made of precious metal: it is often simply called 'the silver' or 'the gold'. In Norway it was called *bunadsølv*, or costume silver; in France the dowry jewellery was known as the *ors* or *dorures*, and in northern Italy *ori* (gold). It was an important part of the dowry everywhere. The value of traditional jewellery was primarily in the metal, not in the workmanship or stones. Where stones were used, they were usually brightly coloured pastes or inexpensive native gems, such as rock crystal, garnets, coral and fresh-water pearls. The stones were simply polished, or facetted in an often old-fashioned cut. The colour of the stone, when used, was usually more important than the precise material. So if red were an auspicious colour, as it was in many places, a red paste would be just as acceptable as a red gemstone. Traditional jewellery rarely involved expensive techniques, such as cut steel, although imitations of more expensive treatments and materials are frequent (plate 5). Another common element, which was regarded as almost synonymous with traditional jewellery, was filigree (see plate 4). Filigree work was often considered an appropriate occupation for women and children, who provided cheap, dextrous labour. In Germany, the wives and daughters of the silversmiths were often responsible for transforming the carefully measured lengths of wire into filigree scrolls.

The acquisition and use of the jewellery, like everything associated with traditional life, was controlled by unwritten, but rigidly observed, customs. Marriage was the most important occasion for at least the initial acquisition of jewellery almost everywhere. Bridal jewellery was sanctioned by scripture as well as custom, and it would have taken great daring for an unmarried girl to wear something denoting

5   **Pair of earrings**
Gold with enamel, filigree, garnets and pearls, length 6.8cm. Russia, 1800–90. V&A: 221&A–1892

This type of earring first appeared in Russia at the beginning of the eighteenth century, but was restricted to traditional costume by the nineteenth. The details carefully imitate the earlier aristocratic originals, with green enamel for emeralds, and foiled garnets for rubies.

married status in any country in the nineteenth century. In some cases jewellery was passed down from mother to daughter as heirlooms, but in most places at least part had to be bought new for the event. In the Balkans, eastern tradition demanded entirely new jewellery for marriage. Custom varied as to whether the father or the bridegroom paid for the dowry jewellery. It was important for brides to wear as much as possible on their wedding day, and if they had not acquired enough, they often borrowed from family or friends, or even hired it. After the wedding, most of the marriage jewellery continued in use on Sundays and feast days for the rest of the owner's life, augmented over the years by gifts and purchases, if her life were prosperous, or depleted by sales if things went badly. The dowry jewellery provided at marriage almost always belonged to the wife, as her insurance against future financial difficulties.

The majority of this jewellery was intended for women's use. Most traditional cultures in nineteenth-century Europe disapproved of purely ornamental jewellery for men, although they were usually allowed to wear decorative functional items. In previous centuries, their weaponry had been embellished by the same silversmiths who made their wives' jewellery, but by the nineteenth century, the habit of wearing weapons on a daily basis had died out in most of Europe, with the exception of the Balkans (plate 7). Men therefore lavished their wealth and attention on the accessories their traditional dress allowed, such as silver watch chains and signet rings, buckles for shoes, hats or breeches, ring brooches at the neck (plate 6), and,

always, buttons. The latter were the main items of jewellery for men everywhere, and were often worn in extravagant quantities.

The origins of most kinds of traditional jewellery lie in fashionable, usually high-status, jewellery. It is not clear when distinctive regional jewellery first appeared. In northern Europe there are indications in written records that identifiable traditional jewellery was already being worn in some places by the seventeenth century, and Benvenuto Cellini, the sixteenth-century Italian goldsmith, distinguishes between urban and rural peasant jewellery in Italy in his time. An archaic name for a piece of jewellery, in an obscure dialect, can be a good indicator of long usage. Regardless of its origins, it reached its zenith in the nineteenth century, when traditional costume was worn, at least in part, by the majority of the rural population throughout Europe. The peak occurred earlier in the north of Europe, where its use was already beginning to decline by the middle of the century, than in the east, where it continued in widespread use up to the First World War. There is no single common reason why traditional jewellery flourished in some places more than others. Isolation certainly played a part. Cultural and political factors were also important. Traditional costume and jewellery were often conspicuously different among minority groups in a region, particularly when those minorities were rich and protected. Examples include the Transylvanian Saxons (plate 8), and the Dutch Amagers, who lived near Copenhagen. Religious differences were also often marked,

6   **Heart-shaped ring brooch**
    Silver, length 8cm.
    Austria, 1800–30.
    Private collection

This ring brooch was worn by a man to fasten the neck of his shirt or his cravat. He was probably a farmer, judging by the cow at the top and the milk pail hanging from the tip. Heart-shaped brooches were worn by men throughout the German Alpine region, and in much of central Europe.

7 **Man from Obbrovazzo, Dalmatia**
From *Dalmatien und seine Volkskunst*,
N. Bruck-Auffenberg
(Vienna, *c*.1900)

This man is posing in a studio in his full traditional dress. He has a bone-hilted *yataghan* in his belt, together with a brace of flintlock pistols, and his waistcoat and jacket are covered with silver buttons in various designs.

especially when different sects lived side by side, as in the Netherlands or Switzerland, although these differences were often more pronounced in costume than in jewellery. Religion was, however, probably the most important influence on the kind of jewellery that was worn. Protestants did not wear earrings, although they were ubiquitous throughout Catholic and Orthodox regions of Europe. Hair pins also were absent in Protestant countries. Large waist clasps are only found in the region of Islamic heritage, the Balkans, and the use of bracelets there may also derive from Islamic or Byzantine tradition. This is not to imply that these practices were directly dictated by the religious authorities. Many reasons are given for wearing earrings in those countries in which they are worn, but none is connected to orthodox belief. It is simply that earrings are not found with traditional costume in Protestant communities.

One of the most interesting aspects of European traditional jewellery is its influence on traditional jewellery outside the continent. This is most marked in Latin America, where Hispanic models have wiped out almost all trace of pre-Columbian design, but it can also be seen in the jewellery of the Woodlands Indians of North America (plate 9), the low-country jewellery of Sri Lanka, and much urban and tribal jewellery in the Maghreb in north Africa, as well as in the details of design and manufacture in many places in southeast Asia. In each case the initial influence rapidly evolved into something new and original.

The only country without any traditional costume was England. The English attributed this absence to the superiority of the British Constitution, but they liked to see other people wearing theirs. The economic importance of British tourism in Europe in the nineteenth century helped to ensure the use and display of traditional costumes where they survived, and in some countries, including Switzerland, Norway and the Netherlands, new 'national' costumes were created to fulfil British expectations.

Possibly because of the lack of a distinctive costume of their own, fashionable English women envied and admired those which remained in use elsewhere, and collected and wore the traditional jewellery from those countries. This fashion was at its height in the second half of the nineteenth century. Henry Cole, the director of the South Kensington Museum, as the V&A was then known, had been buying traditional jewellery for the Museum since the late 1850s. It fitted perfectly with his aim of acquiring examples of decorative art to improve the quality of design in Britain. By 1872 he had already bought important collections of Italian, Russian, Spanish and Normandy traditional jewellery, as well as a selection of individual pieces from various countries at the French International Exhibition of 1867 (see plate 163). To help balance the collection, he persuaded the British Foreign Minister to send a circular to embassies and consulates around the world in 1871, asking them to collect examples of traditional peasant jewellery from their regions. These would be shown first at the International Exhibition to be held in London in 1872, and would then be transferred to

8 **Woman's belt**
Silver-gilt with turquoises and coloured pastes on cloth, length 113cm. Transylvania, Romania, 1750–1850.
V&A: M.18–1953 (Given by Dr W.L. Hildburgh)

The marriage belt was one of the most visible and ostentatious signs of identity for Transylvanian Saxon women. It was worn wrapped around the waist, so that the two decorative ends lay side by side at the front (see plate 66).

9 Paul Kane, *Ke-Wah-Ten*
or *The North Wind*, 1861
Stark Museum of Art,
Orange, Texas

Both men and women
of the North American
Woodlands tribes wore
large numbers of ring
brooches of European
origin. This woman is
wearing plain round
brooches, star-shaped
brooches and a French
Catholic cross. Other
popular types of ring
brooch in the region
included hearts and
Masonic designs.

10 Clasp
Silver and niello, width
22cm. Albania, 1870–80.
Private collection

Clasps such as this were
worn by women in Epirus –
now in Greece, but part of
Albania in the nineteenth
century – to fasten their
clothing (see plate 1).
The design was registered
in Britain in 1873 and
enjoyed great success for
several years. This clasp
was probably made and
imported at that time.

**11 Advertisement for
W.H. Thornhill,
Christmas, 1874**
From *The Queen*,
12 December 1874

W.H. Thornhill was the
leading London retailer of
fashionable accessories.
The 'Albanian belt' (bottom)
is a variation of his
successful 'Norwegian belt'
(top centre) featuring an
Albanian clasp. Surviving
examples show that the
Albanian clasps appear to
have been imported, as they
are unmarked, while all
the other silver fittings on
the belt have full English
silver marks.

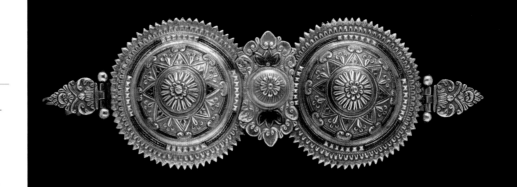

the South Kensington Museum to go on permanent display. Around 500 items were eventually acquired as a result of this initiative, mostly from Europe, but also from India and South America.

The visual impact of this jewellery, first at the Exhibition, and more importantly afterwards at the Museum, provided an important stimulus to interest in traditional jewellery in England. Columnists for women's magazines, such as *The Queen*, filled their pages with reports and engraved illustrations of the pieces on show. Readers responded with requests for information on how and where they could buy such jewellery for themselves, closely followed by advertisements from retailers providing the required information. It is clear from these ads that much of the European peasant jewellery worn in England in the nineteenth century, and still to be found today in antique shops and markets, was imported wholesale in response to consumer demand at the time, not casually and individually by tourists or immigrants (plates 10 and 11). Some specific pieces, such as the Breton necklet in 1873–4 (plate 12), became essential fashion items for a season or so, but peasant jewellery in general was regarded as desirable and fashionable throughout most of the second half of the nineteenth century in Britain. This does not seem to have been the case elsewhere in Europe, or in the USA, where most of the traditional jewellery which survives was brought in piecemeal by immigrants, and consequently never achieved fashionable status.

12 'Breton necklet'
Black velvet with gilt metal appliqués, length (at front) 20cm. Macon, France, 1865–70.
V&A: 1237–1873

The 'Breton necklet' has the same components as other French cross pendants, but the cross and slide are sewn to the ribbon, which is also richly decorated with gilt appliqués of various shapes. It was worn in various provinces of France, but also enjoyed great popularity in Britain in the early 1870s.

13 Belt
Cast and pierced silver,
length 104.1cm. South
Germany, 1650–1750.
V&A: M.34–1939
(May Morris Bequest)

This belt is a traditional
south German marriage
belt, slightly altered to
make it more suitable
for an English wearer. It
belonged to William Morris'
wife Janey, who can be
seen wearing it in the 1877
painting *Astarte Syriaca* by
the Pre-Raphaelite artist
Dante Gabriel Rossetti.

14 Necklace (*Hopfenkette*)
Silver-gilt filigree set with
amethysts and a pendent
pearl, length 34cm.
Nuremberg, south Germany,
1800–50.
V&A: M.230–1925
(Gift of Miss Lucy I. Barlow)

The *Hopfenkette*, or 'hop
chain' necklace, is typical
of Nuremberg. T. Oldham
Barlow brought this one
back from Germany, slightly
altered, as a present for
his daughter. He also lent
it to the artist John Everett
Millais, who used it in his
1878 painting *The Princes
in the Tower*.

The demand for authentic peasant jewellery by fashionable young women also had consequences for British manufacturers, although possibly not quite as Henry Cole had envisaged. From around 1870 onwards, many of the main silverware companies in Birmingham and London produced direct imitations of the most fashionable articles. The peasant jewellery collections at the South Kensington Museum had a more important influence on the artistic community. The Pre-Raphaelites liked the often archaic and unusual appearance of traditional jewellery (plate 13); they dressed their womenfolk in it, and used it extensively in their paintings (plates 14 and 15). The jewellers of the Arts and Crafts movement valued it, as they did the jewellery of the Middle Ages and the Renaissance, for its roots in a pre-industrial world, where hand skills still had pride of place.

Although traditional jewellery largely lost its appeal among the general population in the early twentieth century, it has always remained popular with art students, and still retains its ability to surprise and inspire today.

15 **John Everett Millais,**
The Princes in the Tower
Oil on canvas, 1878. Royal Holloway College, University of London/The Bridgeman Art Library

The older prince is wearing a *Hopfenkette* necklace from Nuremberg, the rich and exotic appearance of which perfectly matched the artist's idea of medieval jewellery.

The Nordic Region

From Iceland through Scotland and Scandinavia to Finland, the Baltic States and parts of northwest Russia

The Nordic region stretches in a wide arc from Iceland in the Atlantic through Scandinavia to Finland and northwest Russia in the east. On its way, it broadens to include the Highlands of Scotland, whose traditional jewellery is firmly part of this region. The jewellery of all these places clearly shares a common cultural origin, although this has developed differently in different places.

Nordic jewellery tends to follow late medieval forms and functions. It was made to accompany a woman's costume which primarily consisted of a plain shift, topped by a full skirt and laced bodice or jacket, with outer garments and cloaks to keep out the cold. In some places, most conspicuously Iceland, women added a decorative apron on formal occasions.

Traditional jewellery from the Nordic region is almost always made of silver, rather than gold, although partial gilding is common. Women's jewellery was mostly worn on the upper part of the dress, and consisted of ring brooches and other fasteners of various kinds, as well as finger rings and chains (plate 16). It was not until the late nineteenth century that items such as earrings and bracelets appeared, but they never became part of traditional dress. Men too wore jewellery to fasten their clothing, using decorative buttons as well as ring brooches.

From around 1860, silversmiths throughout the region, led by Norwegians such as Jacob Tostrup and David Andersen in Oslo and Marius Hammer in Bergen, started to make jewellery using traditional styles and techniques, particularly filigree, but in shapes and designs more suited to the urban dress of the

16 **Bridal pair from Setesdal, Norway, *c*.1852**
From *Norske Nationaldragter*, Christian Tønsberg (Christiania, 1852)

The groom is wearing two ring brooches on his shirt, and a pair of linked buttons at his throat. The bride has four large ring brooches down the front of her costume, a bridal pendant on a long chain, and a *støle* belt, as well as large numbers of gilt ornaments on her bodice, numerous rings and a bridal crown.

1

period. This new national revivalist jewellery was welcomed in Norway as much as by foreigners, and was frequently worn with the traditional costumes which became increasingly popular after 1900. It is now often mistaken for true Norwegian traditional jewellery.

There was great respect for tradition throughout the Nordic region. Old jewellery was sometimes handed down from mother to daughter through several generations, as can be seen from the names and dates engraved on it, and traditional jewellery, such as belts, is frequently mentioned in wills. Old silver, sometimes found in the ground or inherited from mythical ancestors, was widely believed to be the work of fairies, due to its quality and the techniques used, which were different from those practised by living silversmiths. It was highly esteemed and held to have protective qualities.

Ring brooches

The most important item of jewellery was the ring brooch. A ring brooch is a brooch with a loose pin, called a tang, attached to one side. It differs from modern brooches in the way it is fastened. The material of the garment is pulled through the frame of the brooch and then pierced with the tang. As the garment settles back into place, the tension of the cloth holds the tang, and consequently the brooch, firmly in place, without any need for further hooks or catches. It is a very old, and secure, way of fastening clothing, which was used universally in Europe in the Middle Ages. In 1571, the Goldsmiths' Company of London, the association responsible for assaying precious metals, chose a ring brooch to epitomize jewellery on its coat of arms. The ring brooch survived until the late nineteenth century as the only kind worn with traditional costume in the Nordic region.

Ring brooches in the Nordic region are usually round or heart-shaped (plate 17), with plain tangs and decorative frames. Norway has the greatest variety. There are well over 50 different words in Norwegian for the various kinds of ring brooch, which are derived from their style, construction and function, as well as the regions where they were used. They were worn by men, women and children, often several at a time, mainly down the front of the chest. Women's are always the most decorative. The most distinctive pattern was the *bolesølje* (plates 18 and 19), with drum-shaped mounts, which was unique to Norway. Other common patterns included the *slangesølje* (plate 20), shaped like a snake, the flat open *rosesølje*, and the archaic *glibbsølje* (plate 21) with little faces round the edge. The richest designs tend to come from the central and southern parts of the country, particularly Telemark, while in the north of Norway the round ring brooches are often curved, like those used across the border in Sweden (plate 22). Heart brooches are more common in Sweden (plate 23) and in eastern Norway. Norwegian ring brooches are often smothered with little pendants shaped like bowls or ears of barley (plate 24), or have long elaborate filigree pendants. These increased in number, size and complexity during the nineteenth century (plate 25).

In Scotland, ring brooches were originally worn only by women, in the traditional Nordic way, to fasten the shift or

17 **Heart-shaped ring brooch**
(*Hjertesølje*)
Silver-gilt, length 4.1cm.
Fredrik Strøm (maker),
Bergen, west Norway, 1847.
Private collection

Heart-shaped brooches are found throughout Norway, and were commonly used as tokens of love. The large top is typical of the kind made in Bergen. Small ring brooches, either round or heart-shaped, were used to fasten the shirt at the neck by men, women and children.

18 Ring brooch (*Bolesølje*)
Cast silver-gilt, diam.
9.9cm. Norway, 1750–1800.
V&A: 38–1894

Bolesøljer take their name
from a medieval cylindrical
box, called a *bole*. The
cast examples usually
pre-date the filigree kind,
and their decoration
remains unchanged since
medieval times.

19 Ring brooch (*Bolesølje*)
Silver-gilt filigree, diam.
8.5cm. Norway, 1750–1800.
V&A: 372–1907

The *bolesølje* was one of
the most expensive and
ostentatious of Norwegian
ring brooches. This is one
of the earliest of the filigree
designs – later brooches
are completely covered
with filigree, and have even
smaller holes in the centre.

20 **Ring brooch (*Slangesølje*)**
Silver-gilt filigree, diam.
9.7cm. Tor Grinderud
(maker), Lunde, south
Norway, *c*.1850.
V&A: 1335–1873

The *slangesølje*, or snake
brooch, was the most
popular kind in Telemark.
They are all filigree in
design, although the oldest
are made of cast imitation
filigree. Tor Grinderud,
working between 1825
and 1870, was a leading
maker of traditional
Telemark jewellery.

21 **Ring brooch (*Glibbsølje*)**
Cast silver-gilt, diam. 5cm.
1800–99.
V&A: M.54–1955
(Given by Dr W.L. Hildburgh)

The *glibbsølje* derives its
name from the six faces
round its edge. Mainly
found in the western
regions, as far north as
Lapland, the cast design
is probably medieval in
origin, but cannot be
traced back directly.

22 **Ring brooch (*Bröstsölja*)**
Silver, diam. 4.7cm.
A.G. Millberg (maker),
Stockholm, Sweden, *c*.1870.
V&A: 1359–1873

The smooth curved shape
of this ring brooch is typical
of Dalarna, in central
Sweden. Similar ring
brooches, called *bursøljer*
or *bursringer*, were worn
in neighbouring Norway.
This brooch was made in
Stockholm by A.G. Millberg,
who specialized in jewellery
in traditional style.

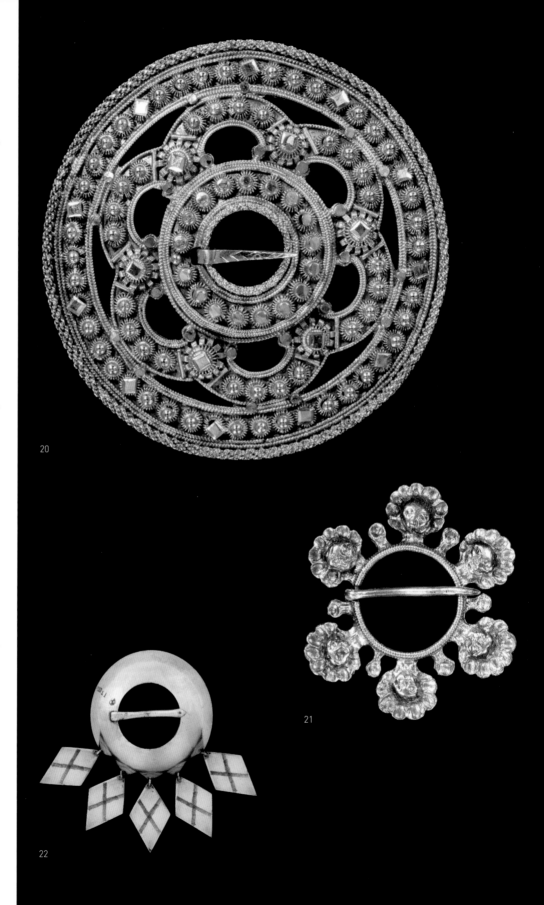

20

21

22

24

25

23 **Heart-shaped ring brooch (*Bröstsölja*)**
Silver filigree set with red pastes, length 5.3cm. P.M. Wallengren (maker), Ystad, Skåne, Sweden, *c.*1850.
V&A: 521–1886

Heart-shaped ring brooches were the most common type in Sweden. The filigree work and red pastes on this brooch are typical of traditional jewellery from Skåne in the south of Sweden. Similar brooches are found in Agder in southern Norway.

24 **Ring brooch (*Byggkornring*)**
Silver filigree, length 8.1cm. PN (maker), Norway, 1870–90.
Private collection

The *byggkornring* is named for its numerous pendants, shaped like ears of barley. Large numbers cover the whole front of the brooch and are typical of Norwegian ring brooches in the late nineteenth century.

25 **Ring brooch (*Hornring*)**
Silver with filigree pendants, length 10.7cm. Telemark, Norway, 1870–90.
Private collection

The *hornring* was originally a plain ring brooch with cast decoration added at the sides, top and bottom. Filigree started to replace the cast decoration in the late eighteenth century. This design, with elaborate pendants of crosses, bowls and points, is typical of the end of the nineteenth century.

shawl (plate 26). From the late eighteenth century, with the development of a romantic, and not always strictly accurate, view of Scotland's cultural history, large round ring brooches were increasingly adopted as part of the male Highland and military costume, where they were worn on the shoulder to fasten the plaid. Many Scottish ring brooches were made in Inverness, but also further south in urban centres such as Edinburgh. The traditional heart-shaped Scottish ring brooch is often called a luckenbooth brooch (plate 27), after the stalls where they were sold in Edinburgh. Scottish ring brooches were also carried across the Atlantic to North America by early settlers. These brooches appealed to the Woodlands tribes, both men and women, who received them in exchange for furs and wore them in often extravagant quantities to decorate their outer dress (see plate 9). Most were made by local silversmiths, although the Hudson's Bay Company imported large quantities of trade silver jewellery from London makers, such as the Bateman family, in the late eighteenth and early nineteenth centuries.

In Finland (plate 28), and along the Baltic coast, ring brooches were often the only element of traditional jewellery to survive into the nineteenth century. They could be immensely large, covering the whole front of a woman's dress. In the Baltic states of Latvia and Estonia, the native peoples preserved their sense of identity during Soviet times with costumes, song and dance, and the ring brooches they wore were an essential part of this costume (plate 29). During that period, they were more commonly made of *melchior* (base) metal, than silver, but the

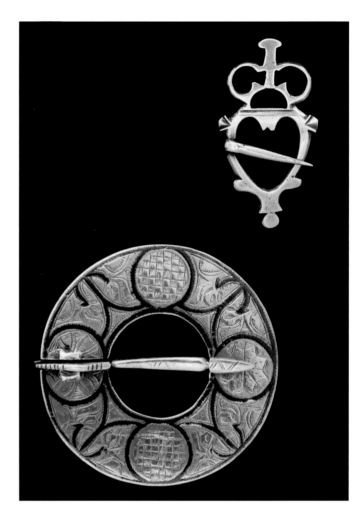

26 **Ring brooch**
Silver and niello, diam. 7.1cm. Scotland, 1769. V&A: M.13–1972

This large ring brooch was used to fasten a woman's shawl. The loops and rings of the design are a late development of the Celtic interlace pattern which was popular in the second half of the eighteenth century. The initials and date scratched on the back suggest it was probably a betrothal gift.

27 **Heart-shaped ring brooch (Luckenbooth brooch)**
Cast silver, length 4.1cm. C. Jamieson (maker), Inverness, Scotland, *c*.1800. V&A: M.809–1926 (Lt. Col. G.B. Croft-Lyons Bequest)

Heart-shaped ring brooches for women, often called luckenbooth brooches, were given as love tokens in Scotland, and were also believed to have protective qualities. Many were made in Inverness, the main town of the Highland region.

traditional designs were faithfully copied and maintained.

Ring brooches function best with loose, homespun cloths, such as the linen and wool which were the main traditional clothing materials in the region. The strong tangs tear apart more tightly woven cloths, such as cotton or silk, and stretch or damage tailored clothing. As fashionable dress gradually replaced traditional costume, their owners could no longer wear their old ring brooches. Many were reluctant to give them up completely, and often had modern brooch fittings added at the back. Photographs of Norwegian immigrants in America show that they often retained their ring brooch long after they had ceased to wear any other trace of traditional costume.

Bodice fasteners and clasps

In addition to the ring brooch, various kinds of bodice fasteners and other clasps featured in women's dress in most countries in the Nordic region. The bodice fasteners were usually worn in pairs down the front of the dress, a dozen or more at a time (plate 31). The earliest and most basic, colloquially called *fiskmaljor* (fish clasps) in Sweden because of their shape, were small cast plaques with a hole at one end (plate 30). This type, with a hole at one end, is also found in Iceland. The holes faced each other across the bodice opening and were originally laced tight with a string or leather cord; this was often replaced in traditional costume by a silver chain, with a stiff silver bodkin, or tag, at each end. From the late eighteenth century onwards, bodice fasteners were increasingly made of filigree (plate 32). In Norway, particularly in the Telemark region, the filigree bodice

| 28 | **Ring brooch** | 29 | **Ring brooch (*Sakta*)** |

28 **Ring brooch**
Silver, diam. 9.1cm. Vipuri,
Finland (now Vyborg,
Russia), 1862.
Private collection

Vipuri is in the former
Finnish province of Karelia.
Ring brooches from Karelia,
now in Russia, are similar to
those from Estonia, and can
be very large. This one has
the Finnish date letter for
1862 (E3) and the Russian
78 zolotnik standard mark.

29 **Ring brooch (*Sakta*)**
Silver, diam. 10cm.
South Kurzeme, Latvia.
*c.*1900.
Private collection

By the nineteenth century,
ring brooches in Latvia
were worn only by women.
They used small ones to
fasten the neck of their
shirt, and large ones, such
as this, to secure their
shawl at the front. *Saktas*
are still being made in
this design, although now
rarely in silver.

fasteners were circular, with the lacing hole at one side (plate 33). In some areas, bodice clasps, which hooked directly into each other, replaced the ring-shaped fasteners, and these became increasingly interchangeable with jacket and belt clasps (plate 34). By the nineteenth century, clasps from the rich farming district of Skåne, in Sweden, had become much larger and purely decorative (plate 35). They were increasingly made of thin stamped sheet silver decorated with coloured pastes, and moved away from the edge of the bodice to become ornamental plaques across its front (see plate 42).

In Lapland, in the north of the region, where Norway, Sweden, Finland and Russia meet within the Arctic Circle, the nomadic Sami deer herders put all their surplus wealth into silver – mainly jewellery and spoons. They did not make it themselves, but bought it at the fairs held annually in places such as Lofoten, in northern Norway. Most of the oldest Lapp silver was made at Bergen, where the northern trade was an important part of the silversmith's business in the seventeenth century. From the eighteenth century onwards work by silversmiths from the north of Sweden and Finland predominated. Traditional Lapp jewellery resembles that worn by women elsewhere in the region, as it was made by the same silversmiths, but there are often subtle differences. The Sami would only buy silver which matched their precise requirements regarding technique and appearance. They also wore it differently: Sami women sewed their silver onto a decorative yoke, richly ornamented with a mass of buttons, appliqués, bodice fasteners and clasps (plate 36).

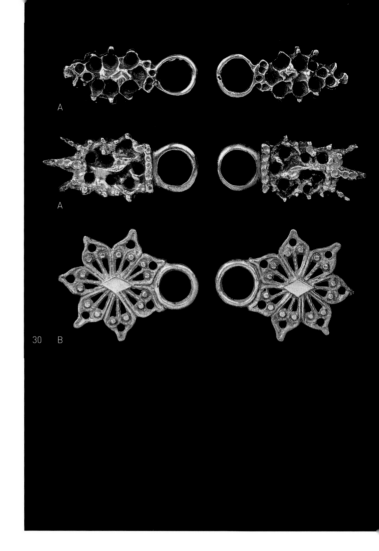

30	**Bodice fasteners**	31	**Bodice fasteners** (*Maljor*)
	Cast silver		Cast silver-gilt, diam.
A	width 3.3cm, Norway or		2.2cm. Sweden, c.1840.
	Sweden, 1800–99.		V&A: 544–1886
	Private Collection		
B	width 3cm, Iceland,		
	1800–70.		
	V&A: 361&A–1870		

Bodice fasteners were worn in matching pairs down the front opening of the bodice. The Renaissance design of a winged angel's head is found on many kinds of Swedish traditional jewellery.

Small cast silver eyelets, with a hole at one end for the lace, are the earliest kind of bodice fastener. Their design dates back to the Middle Ages. Cast imitation filigree jewellery in the Nordic region is, perversely, often older than true filigree.

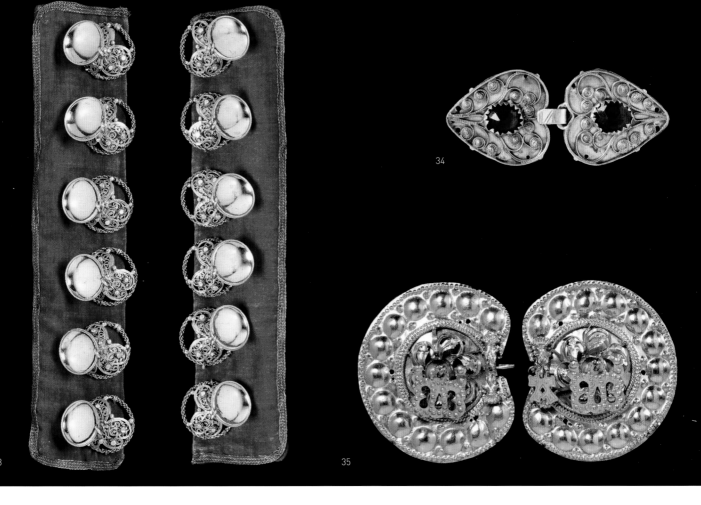

32   **Bodice fasteners**
Sheet silver, partly gilded,
with filigree and red
pastes, diam. 4.1cm.
P.M. Wallengren (maker),
Ystad, Sweden, 1830–79.
V&A: 533H and I–1886

Large bodice fasteners,
made of thin sheet silver
lavishly decorated with
gilding, filigree and
coloured pastes, were
purely ornamental and
far too fragile to have
laced a bodice.

33   **Set of 12 bodice fasteners**
(*Maljer*)
Silver-gilt filigree mounted
on red velvet, length 21cm.
Telemark, Norway, 1800–70.
V&A: 1328–1873

The word *malje* means
eyelet, referring to both
its shape and role. These
bodice fasteners were
worn on the front of a
festive dress, and had an
accompanying silver chain
to lace them together.
Telemark traditional
jewellery is characterized
by a sophisticated use
of filigree.

34   **Jacket clasp**
Silver filigree set with blue
pastes, width 7.1cm.
J. Wahlberg (maker), Ystad,
Skåne, Sweden, 1855.
V&A: 457–1886

Ystad was one of the main
centres for traditional
jewellery in Skåne, which
had the richest tradition
of jewellery in Sweden in
the nineteenth century.
Ystad jewellers specialized
in filigree, often set with
coloured pastes. The blue
paste in this clasp is typical
of their work.

35   **Jacket clasp**
Sheet silver, partly gilded,
width 15.4cm. J. Aspelin
the elder (maker), Ystad,
Sweden, *c.*1800.
V&A: 393–1886

This clasp was purely
decorative. It is made of thin
sheet silver, partly gilded,
to make it as large and
impressive as possible.
The stylized images of
the Virgin Mary over the
fastening, and the Gothic
letter pendants, are late
medieval Catholic motifs.

Belts

The small clasps worn on the bodice were sometimes repeated, in larger size, to fasten the belt. A woman's belt had important symbolic meaning throughout the Nordic region, and was closely associated with marital status. The earliest pattern is based on the ostentatious belts which were used by the upper classes throughout Europe at the end of the Middle Ages. These medieval belts consisted of a row of decorative plaques sewn to a lavishly embroidered cloth facing on a leather belt, with a large cast buckle. They were much longer than necessary for purely functional reasons, and were designed to allow the decorative end to hang down at the front of the dress.

Over time, these aristocratic belts were absorbed into traditional dress in the Nordic region, and the long end became separate from the belt itself, and developed into a strip of material sewn vertically to the front of the belt. At the same time the heavy Renaissance-style cast plaques changed to smaller, usually square, stamped appliqués, which were sewn round the belt (plate 37) and also on the strip at the front. The pronged buckle often became a hooked clasp, of similar design to those on the bodice. Belts like this are best known from Lapland, where they sometimes retained the long integral end, but they were also part of women's costume in many areas of Norway and Sweden. In Iceland, the belt was made of silver plaques, sewn to a cloth belt or hinged together, and usually made of filigree (plate 38).

In Lapland everyone wore decorative belts, but elsewhere they were only worn by women. Men's traditional belts were

36   Illustration of a Sami woman's decorated collar (*Silverkrage*)
From 'Peasant art in Sweden, Lapland and Iceland', *The Studio*, 1910

The nomadic Sami women wore their surplus silver on a bib tucked into the neck of their dress. Onto this they sewed a profusion of appliqués, clasps and buttons. Lapp silver is almost all late medieval in character, and often slightly different from similar pieces worn by women further south in Norway and Sweden.

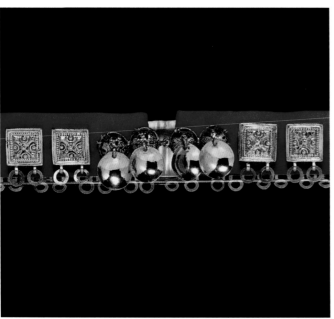

37 **Belt (*Stølebelt*)**
Silver-gilt on red cloth,
length 34cm. Norway,
1800–70.
V&A: 1330–1873

These belts descend directly
from late medieval wedding
belts, and were worn by
women throughout the
Nordic region at marriage
and on special occasions.
The clasp is made from
filigree bodice fasteners,
while the word *støle*
refers to the applied silver
plaques.

38 **Woman's belt**
Silver filigree on black
velvet, length 92cm. Iceland,
1800–50.
V&A: 465–1901

The decoration on this belt
is typical of Icelandic filigree
which has been made there
continuously since medieval
times. It was revived for
traditional jewellery in
the nineteenth century.
Icelandic traditional silver
jewellery was rarely marked
until the late nineteenth
century, as there was no
legal requirement.

more functional, decorated only with base metal clasps and hooks, or occasional embroidery. Sami men's belts, from Lapland, were renowned for their lavish use of tin-thread embroidery. In the north of Norway the men's leather belt was often split into sections, linked by metal rings from which knives and other useful appendages could be hung. When one of these belts was imported into Britain, it inspired the fashionable Bond Street retailer, W.H. Thornhill, to create his 'Norwegian belt' in 1870 (see plate 11). This became one of his most successful accessories, and sold in large numbers over the next thirty years, in various designs and qualities, and was copied by numerous other silversmiths. It survived well into the twentieth century as the belt worn by Scouts and Guides.

Headdresses

The most important event in a woman's life was her wedding, and it was customary to wear as much jewellery as possible at the event, which often lasted for several days (plate 39). Most of this jewellery continued in use during the rest of her life, on Sundays and special occasions, but some pieces were only worn on the day itself. The most important of these was the headdress, which was worn throughout the region to demonstrate the purity of the bride, and the change in her status. The most impressive wedding headdress was a crown, which is still often used today in some parts of Norway in the marriage ceremony. It was usually late medieval or Renaissance in design, reminiscent of the crowns worn by statues of the Virgin in pre-Reformation churches. In Norway,

39 **Adolph Tidemand,
Watercolour of a bride from
Hallingdal, Norway, 1849**
Nasjonalmuseet, Norway

Adolph Tidemand
encountered seventeen-
year-old Ingeborg
Andersdatter on her way to
her wedding in 1849, and
drew this picture. She is
wearing her full wedding
finery: two *støle* belts,
two marriage pendants,
a *bringesølv* plastered
with silver and a gilded
wedding crown tied on
firmly with red ribbons.

40 Bridal crown (*Brudekrone*)
Silver-gilt, height 13.5cm.
Bergen, west Norway,
1650–1750.
V&A: 2–1879

Bridal crowns were worn
mainly in the west of
Norway, although brides
everywhere wore some kind
of special headdress.
It signified the bride's
virginity, by its resemblance
to the crowns worn by
images of the Virgin Mary.
All the decoration has
symbolic value: the lions
stand for strength, the birds
fertility, and the hanging
leaves help to avert evil.

41 Woman's diadem
Silver-gilt filigree, length
39cm. Iceland, 1850–1900.
Private collection

The diadem was adopted
into Icelandic traditional
dress in the middle of
the nineteenth century,
replacing an earlier cap
with a silver tube and tassel.
These diadems were made
of silver filigree appliqués
attached to a black velvet
band, or a hinged band of
solid filigree.

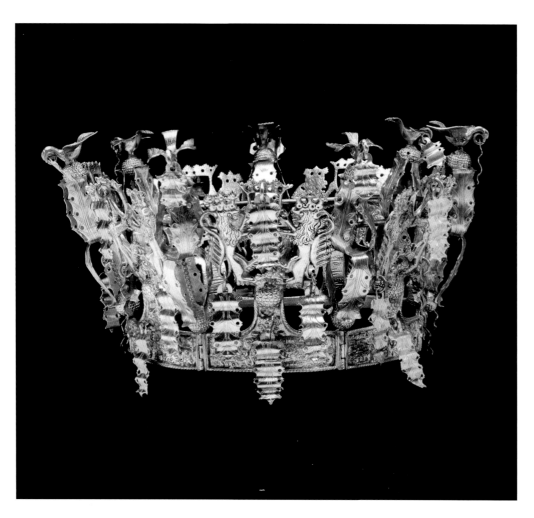

these crowns were often very heavy, sometimes causing the bride to faint from the weight. The example shown (plate 40) weighs well over one kilo, which is heavier than the British Imperial State Crown. Few brides were rich enough to own one, and in Norway most rented one from a wealthier neighbour, paying with embroidered ribbons or some other personal service as often as with money.

Swedish wedding crowns were originally as large and heavy as those worn in Norway, but from the late eighteenth century onwards they were often reduced in size to become small coronets worn on the top of the head. These were usually owned and rented out by the parish church, rather than by rich individuals; in the sixteenth century, the Swedish Synod, disturbed by the number of couples who did not bother to get married in church, instructed the clergy to melt down any old unused church silver to make into wedding crowns, to increase the attraction of a church wedding.

Brides always wore some kind of special headdress at their wedding, even if full crowns were not customary. The oldest design was a stiff construction of cloth, called a *lad* in Norwegian, which was covered all over with silver appliqués, buttons and bodice fasteners. These were worn in many places throughout Norway and Sweden, and probably in Denmark before the nineteenth century, sometimes as well as, rather than instead of, the wedding crown.

In Iceland, some pieces of traditional jewellery developed quite differently from those in the rest of the region. The most unusual was a short silver tube with a long tassel hanging out of it, which was worn on a cap on the head. This must have been of very early use in Iceland; it was considered the most important item of jewellery for women, and even the poorest would wear one, even if they could not afford any other jewellery. In the middle of the nineteenth century it was replaced by a filigree diadem (plate 41) when a new traditional costume was adopted.

Necklaces and pendants

Necklaces were not common in traditional Nordic dress, and those that did exist mostly consisted of long chains holding pendants. The main exception is in Skåne, in the extreme south of Sweden, where choker necklaces, made of parallel chains with a large clasp at the front decorated with filigree and coloured pastes, were common (plate 43). They were probably introduced from Germany in the mid-eighteenth century. It was common for Swedish silversmiths to undertake part of their training abroad, and similar choker necklaces were worn in the Alpine regions of Upper Austria (see plate 78), Bavaria and Switzerland (see plate 77). In addition to this choker, Skåne women wore elegant pendants carrying religious monograms and depictions of winged angels' heads and the crucifixion (plate 42). It may seem strange to find Catholic religious iconography surviving so prominently in a Protestant country, but Swedish Lutheranism was always more accommodative than the 'black' Calvinism of some parts of mainland Europe. Swedish religious pendants are called *kors* (cross), regardless of their shape. Among the most common are large tau crosses

42   **Bridal couple in Skåne costume**
From *Et år i Sverige*,
A. Grafstrom
(Stockholm, 1827)

This bride is wearing an IHS pendant and tau cross, large jacket ornaments on red rosettes, a gilt neck clasp, and a spherical button hanging from her sleeve. The traditional jewellery worn in Skåne was richer and more profuse than in any other region of the country.

43 **Necklace (*Halslås*)**
Silver filigree set with red
pastes, length 39.5cm.
Gabriel Dahlberg (maker),
Lund, Sweden, 1850.
V&A: 381–1886

Necklaces first appeared in
Skåne in the late eighteenth
century and rapidly spread
through the district to
become one of the most
conspicuous parts of the
costume. Gabriel Dahlberg
was one of the many Skåne
silversmiths who specialized
in traditional jewellery.

44 **Tau cross pendant
(*Striglakors*)**
Silver filigree set with
clear pastes, length 14cm.
N. Bleckberg (maker),
Karlshamn, Sweden, *c.*1800.
V&A: 376–1886

The tau cross is a T-shaped
cross which is typical of
southern Sweden, and is not
found in traditional jewellery
elsewhere. The pastes on
this example were originally
backed with red foil, but
the colour has faded over
time so they now appear
colourless.

45 **Religious pendant
(*Sållakors*)**
Silver, partly gilded, length
8.6cm. Lund, Skåne,
Sweden, 1750–1800.
V&A: 415–1886

The word *sållakors* means
a sieve cross (the word
kors (cross) was used for
all religious pendants).
The sieve is formed from
a pierced monogram
of the letters 'IHS'. The
little Gothic monogram
represents the first words of
the Latin prayer 'Ave Maria'.

43

44

(plate 44) and circular discs, often stamped with an image of the crucifixion or pierced to reveal the sacred monogram IHS (plate 45), which represents the first three letters of the name Jesus in Greek. They were all hung profusely with the shallow dish pendants found throughout Scandinavia, whose tinkling sound was intended to avert the devil.

Similar religious pendants, called *angstei*, were worn by Norwegian women, but only on their wedding day. By the nineteenth century they had lost all traces of their religious origin and were purely decorative (plate 46), but the name reveals their previous function; they had originally contained a wax disc stamped with an image of the paschal lamb, the *Agnus Dei*.

There is little evidence for the wearing of non- or pre-Christian amulets in Nordic traditional jewellery, although belief in the protective powers of metal and stone undoubtedly survived. Some medieval jewels in Scotland were used as charms to cure illness, for both humans and animals, and the little heart-shaped ring brooches worn there were widely believed to promote lactation and to protect the new-born from witches. They are sometimes known as witches brooches as a result. Norwegian mothers attached small pieces of silver, preferably inherited, such as ring brooches, to their babies' clothing, to protect them from being stolen by the fairies. In Sweden, elaborate instructions survive for the making of a silver *tigge* cross, a tiny amulet the size and shape of a penny, to protect against evil spirits and disease, and details in silversmiths' accounts show that these medallions were

46 **Marriage pendant (*Brudedaler*)**
Silver filigree, partly gilded, length 13.4cm.
West Norway, 1800–99.
V&A: M.54-1939
(Given by Mrs A.E. Gunter)

The *brudedaler* was worn by the bride at her wedding. The name means a bridal coin, and many were originally made from large silver coins. It is also sometimes called an *angstei*, or *Agnus Dei*, because it originally contained an image of the Lamb of God.

47 Ring (*Dragering*)
Silver-gilt, diam. 2.7cm.
Bergen, west Norway,
1750–1850.
Private collection

The *dragering* is shaped like
a stylized dragon wrapped
round the finger, and was
worn mainly in the west of
Norway. It usually has little
pendants of rings or bowls,
whose tinkling sound as the
hand moved was believed to
avert evil spirits.

48 Ring (*Lappring*)
Silver-gilt, diam. 2.1cm.
J.E. Pettersson (maker),
Gällivare, Sweden, 1896.
Private collection

Rings with numerous
pendent ringlets are
usually known as Lapp
wedding rings, although by
the end of the nineteenth
century they were produced
commercially in many
places in Sweden. This one
was made by John Erik
Pettersson, a silversmith
living in Lapland who
specialized in Sami
traditional jewellery.

49 Ring
Sheet silver set with
red, orange and blue
pastes, diam. 2.9cm. A.R.
Flinkenberg (maker),
Simrishamn, Skåne,
Sweden, 1820–66.
V&A: 484–1886

Rings of thin sheet silver
set with coloured pastes
appeared at the beginning
of the nineteenth century,
but were largely replaced
by rings with little pendent
ringlets by the latter half
of the century. They were
mainly worn by women.

actually made. Similar traditions survive in Norway. The
natural protective qualities of a piece of amber (see plate 2)
would have been enhanced by the image of the crucifixion and
the IHS monogram on its mount.

Rings

Traditional finger rings in Norway and Sweden are usually
wide bands decorated with small pendent dishes or rings.
In Norway, there are only three to six pendants, hanging in a
horizontal row from the front of the ring (plate 47). In Sweden,
the ringlets are smaller, and there are more of them, arranged
on a lozenge-shaped bezel (plate 48). Earlier, Swedish rings
were decorated with coloured pastes (plate 49), but by the end
of the nineteenth century the rings with little ringlets were
predominant. They are often described as Lapp wedding rings,
but were originally worn over a much wider area. By 1900 they
were listed as *lapprings* in the catalogue of the Swedish mail
order firm Åhlén & Holm.

Buttons

The earliest kind of button in the region was large, hollow
and spherical, decorated with circles of applied wire, which
descended directly from those worn as women's sleeve
ornaments in the Middle Ages. These survived in common
use in Iceland and Lapland, and in Skåne in southern Sweden
(plate 50), until the end of the nineteenth century. Elsewhere
the earliest buttons were collar links. These were pairs of
buttons, joined together by a link, which fastened the neck

50 Button
Silver, partly gilded, diam.
2.7cm. E. Holmberg
(maker), Lund, Skåne,
Sweden, 1774–1819.
V&A: 468A–1886

Large round buttons, often
with pendants, are late
medieval in origin. They
were worn decoratively by
women in Skåne along the
lower seam of their jacket
sleeve. In Lapland, they
were worn on the collar,
together with all the other
dress silver.

opening of the shirt. In Norway, they were often huge open filigree buttons, either fully spherical, or with a flat back. Collar links frequently had decorative pendants: Gothic letters representing religious monograms in Sweden and Lapland, and long complex filigree chains in Norway (plate 51). Cuff links were similar, but appeared later, and never featured pendants.

In Lapland, traditional buttons were only worn by women, as appliqués on their decorative yokes. It was not until the eighteenth century that men in the Nordic region started to add functional buttons to their clothing, and women did not use buttons as dress fasteners until well into the nineteenth century. These dress buttons are usually flat, with engraved patterns or applied filigree. Flat buttons, decorated with a stylized engraved flower and worn by men, are almost the only kind of traditional jewellery which survives from Denmark.

The largest and most decorative buttons developed in Iceland. As well as the other types used throughout the Nordic region, Icelandic women wore three special buttons, shaped like little drums or pill boxes (plate 52), on the waistband of their apron. The earliest were made of sheet silver with repoussé decoration, but the most characteristic are of open filigree, over a protective back plate. Icelandic filigree has a strong, distinctive, often slightly asymmetric character which recalls medieval interlace design. This filigree jewellery was much admired in England in the nineteenth century, and must have been imported commercially given the amount which still survives, as Iceland was not a major tourist centre at the time.

---

51 **Collar stud (*Dingsilknapp*)**
Silver filigree, length
14.9cm. Gudbrandsdal,
central Norway, 1800–70.
V&A: 656–1872

Stud buttons were worn,
as an alternative to collar
links, to fasten the shirt
at the neck. Those with
fancy pendants were
usually worn by women.
The longest and most
decorative filigree stud
pendants come from
Gudbrandsdal in central
Norway.

52 **Apron button
(*Samfelluhnappur*)**
Silver filigree, diam. 3.8cm.
Iceland, 1800–70.
V&A: 621–1872

Icelandic women wore
three large buttons along
the front waistband of their
decorative apron. The apron
did not have strings, but was
held up by a belt, which was
fastened below the buttons.
The buttons prevented the
apron from slipping down.

The Netherlands

The geographical position of the Netherlands, and the economic and political strength which allowed the Dutch to maintain a degree of independence in the political disturbances which swept across northern Europe in the seventeenth century, ensured that their traditional costume and jewellery remained distinct from that of other places, and is, in many cases, unique. Although there are considerable differences between regions, and between Catholic and Protestant costumes, they all retain a distinctively Dutch character. The traditional jewellery of Belgium, and the Frisian areas of north Germany, also belongs in this region.

The waters that helped to isolate the Dutch also provided wealth through fishing and trading. The rich farmers' wives were joined by the wives of seafarers in using expensive or exotic materials, such as chintz for their traditional costumes and gold for their jewellery (plate 53). Another aspect, probably of Calvinist origin, that distinguishes traditional jewellery in the Netherlands is the comparative lack of importance given to wedding jewellery. Although the costumes and jewellery of unmarried women were usually different from those worn when married, the jewellery was not primarily acquired at marriage, and little girls could often wear the full range, if their parents were rich enough. Outside Zeeland, even wedding rings were not of great significance, and women were as likely to wear a silver sewing guard (which acted as a kind of thimble) on their finger, as a wedding ring.

In the nineteenth century, the Netherlands became a favourite tourist destination, particularly for the British. This

53 **Traditional costume at Walcheren, Zeeland, *c*.1850**
From *Nederlandsche kleederdragten*, V. Bing (Utrecht, 1865); reproduced in *Costumes of Holland*, C. Nieuwhoff (Amsterdam, 1985)

These spectators at a tilting match are wearing a full complement of Zeeland jewellery. The men have silver filigree *broekstukken*, collar buttons and watch chains. The women have coral necklaces and gold forehead ornaments and *oorijzers*. The terminals either side of her face show that the little girl is wearing one, as well as silver shoe buckles.

2

led to an increased awareness by the Dutch of the value of their picturesque costumes, and in many places these had become rather exaggerated, to the point of caricature, by the end of the nineteenth century. The Dutch adopted one of the traditional costumes of the little fishing village of Volendam, which had become an international artists' centre by 1880, as an unofficial national costume. There is very little jewellery visible in the archetypal image of a Dutch woman wearing this costume, with its long full skirt, winged cap and clogs, but this superficial view hides a rich variety of gold and silver ornaments worn throughout the country.

Headdresses and hair ornaments

The most striking element of all Dutch women's traditional dress is the *oorijzer* (plate 54). An *oorijzer* (there is no equivalent word in any other language, as no one else uses one – the word literally means 'ear-iron') is a kind of headdress, usually made of gold or silver. It started in the seventeenth century as a simple iron band, used to hold an expensive lace cap safely in place against the force of a North Sea gale. By the nineteenth century the *oorijzer* had developed into an extremely expensive piece of jewellery, sometimes covering the whole head like a helmet, and covered in its turn by one or more additional lace caps and bonnets. It was worn throughout the Netherlands, although the design varied from district to district, and was usually accompanied by additional complementary accessories. Because the *oorijzer* itself was usually completely hidden when worn, decorative terminals were added to the ends to make sure

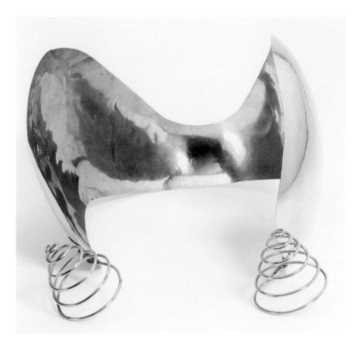

54   *Oorijzer*
Gold, diam. 20cm.
J.M. Boers (maker of part),
Rotterdam, Netherlands,
1841 and 1871.
V&A: 1071:5–1873

Unique to the Netherlands, an *oorijzer* is a headdress which was made to hold a lace cap in place. The spiral ends were made separately from the body, often by different makers. Their shape varies from place to place; these spirals are typical of Zeeland.

that everyone knew it was there (plate 57). These could be flat rectangles, like little books, decorative filigree plaques, or various kinds of rounded knop, but in most places the terminals were spirals.

In pictures, many Dutch women appear to be wearing earrings. In fact, these are usually small pendants, which look like earrings but are hung from the terminal of the *oorijzer* (plate 55, 57). In most cases, the close-fitting *oorijzer* would have made it impossible to wear earrings anyway, but even in those places where the *oorijzer* was no longer worn, women did not wear real earrings. They hooked the pendants into the ends of their cap, above the ear, rather than into the ears themselves, possibly because of a Protestant distaste for ear piercing. Men generally did not wear earrings, or any jewellery that was not strictly functional, with their traditional costume. Seamen, however, often wore a single plain gold earring, which could be justified by the fact that it would pay for a decent Christian burial if they died far from home. In other countries the same practice had a very different explanation (see Chapter 5).

In some regions, Dutch women wore one or two curved plates on their forehead, fastened at one end, under the *oorijzer*, by a small pin (plate 56). The way these were worn was never random, although the precise meaning varied from place to place. In Zeeland, a forehead pin on the left side of the head meant that the wearer was married. If it was on the right side, she was unmarried; her heart, on the left side, was free. Discreet pins held everything firmly in place.

55 **Ear pendants (*Bellen*)**
Gold filigree, length 8.4cm.
A. van Loenen (maker),
Amsterdam, Netherlands,
1830–70.
V&A: 1071:1&2–1873

Few Dutch women wore earrings. These pendants were worn hooked into the spiral ends of the *oorijzer*, and gave the appearance of earrings.

56 **Forehead ornaments (*Zijnaalden*)**
Gold filigree, length 15.5cm.
The Hague, Netherlands,
1856.
V&A: 1071:3&4–1873

Forehead ornaments were worn across the forehead, with the decorative end at the front, and the thin, plain end attached to the headdress by a small pin fastened through the hole. They could be worn in pairs, as here, but were more often used singly.

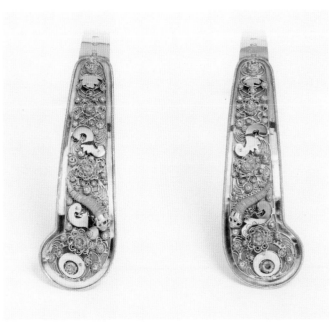

Necklaces and pendants

Only a few traditional costumes in the Netherlands had laced bodices, and those that did were usually covered with a richly decorated breast cloth of some kind. This meant that the main body jewellery for most Dutch women was a choker necklace made from strands of beads with a decorative clasp at the front (plate 57). Red coral was the favourite material, changing to garnets, jet or black glass for mourning (plate 58).

While choker necklaces were almost ubiquitous, crosses were only worn in the Catholic districts and Belgium. Following the Thirty Years' War, the Netherlands was split between the mainly Catholic south, which remained part of the Hapsburg empire and is now Belgium, and the northern United Provinces (the Netherlands) which were independent and Protestant. Despite their identity as a Protestant state, the United Provinces allowed a degree of religious freedom, resulting in a patchwork of different faiths, and these differences were marked at a local level by distinctions in dress and jewellery. In addition to crosses, women in Catholic areas wore long gold chains with delicate filigree plaques, similar to those worn in Emsland in neighbouring German Lower Saxony.

Clasps and buckles

Dutch clasps had a distinctive shape as early as the seventeenth century, with a wide decorative hook which curves forward. They are made of sheet silver or filigree (plate 59), and were used to fasten the outer clothes: cloaks and capes, jackets and aprons. They were originally worn by both men and

57   **A. Spee, portrait of Maria Sandifort-Spee**
The Netherlands, *c*.1850
Courtesy of Piet Minderhoud

Maria Sandifort-Spee is dressed in mourning, with a necklace of dark garnets with a gold clasp. She is also wearing a small pin and a gold *oorijzer* that is concealed by her lace cap so that only its spiral terminals with gold filigree pendants, and the pins which hold it in place, are visible.

58   **Necklace**
Silver set with black pastes and black glass beads, length 44cm. Overijssel, Netherlands, *c*.1900. Private collection

Choker necklaces were worn throughout the Netherlands. This is a mourning necklace, as it is made with black beads and has a silver and black paste clasp. Out of mourning, women preferred coral and gold.

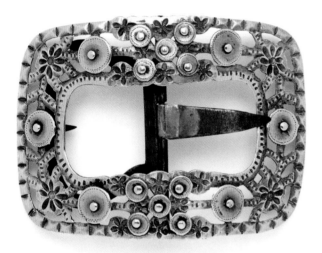

women, but men had ceased to wear them by the nineteenth century. Belt clasps and buckles did not appear until the nineteenth century, when they were mainly worn by women.

Large silver shoe buckles were commonly worn by both sexes (plate 60). Their design was based on those worn by the upper classes in the seventeenth century, but they had developed their own identity by the nineteenth century. They were worn with proper shoes on Sundays and for special occasions; clogs were strictly for working use. Pairs of small buckles, often matching the shoe buckles, were worn to fasten the knee closure of a man's breeches.

Buttons

Dutch women did not wear decorative buttons on their traditional dress before the late nineteenth century; the numerous silver buttons which survive were all made for men. There are two main kinds of Dutch button: round filigree buttons and flat buttons, usually with a pictorial design. Round filigree buttons are common throughout Europe, but the Netherlands is the only place where figural buttons were part of traditional costume.

The design of these buttons, and their place on men's costume, probably dates back to the seventeenth century. Many of the images are based on seventeenth-century coins from the region, and real coins were often made into buttons. Others have political and religious themes, or show horses and riders and agricultural or seafaring images (plate 61). The Calvinist Protestantism of the Netherlands disapproved of any

59 **Clasp (Schortenslot)**
Silver filigree, width 7cm.
Walcheren, Zeeland,
Netherlands, c.1880.
Private collection

This clasp was used to fasten an apron at the back of the waist (see plate 53). Smaller gold clasps of the same design were worn as necklace clasps (kraalhaken) in South Beveland. Towards the end of the nineteenth century, women also started to wear waist buckles made of the same delicate filigree.

60 **Shoe buckle**
Silver and iron, width 9.7cm.
Netherlands, 1901.
Private collection

Large silver shoe buckles were worn by both men and women with their festive costume up to the early twentieth century. The broad triangular tang and the flat silver discs riveted to the surface are typical of Dutch traditional shoe buckles.

61 **Men's pictorial buttons**
Silver.
A Horseman (ruitertje), diam. 2.1cm, R. van der Wolde (maker), Meppel, c.1800. V&A: 8–1892
B Wagon with barrels, diam. 2.4cm, Schoonhoven, 1802. Private collection
C Prince of Orange, diam. 2.4cm, Schoonhoven, 1788. Private collection
D Moses' spies returning from Canaan, diam. 2.5cm, Kingdom of Holland, 1809. V&A: 4–1892
E VOC (Dutch East India Company) ship, W. Koning, Schoonhoven, 1793. Private collection
F Blyheit vryheidt (joy and freedom), diam. 2.4cm, J. van Vlierden (maker), Schoonhoven, 1786. Private collection

A

B

C

D

E

F

62   **Pair of buttons**
      (*Broekstukken*)
      Silver filigree, diam. 9.2cm.
      J.F. de Jonge (maker), Goes,
      Netherlands, 1878–1905.
      Private collection

      Broekstukken were worn
      by men in pairs, joined
      by an oval loop, to fasten
      their breeches. Many
      were converted to belt
      clasps, which were worn
      in the same position,
      when breeches went out
      of fashion. Open filigree
      broekstukken such as these
      are typical of Zeeland.

ostentation in dress, and buttons were one of the few items of jewellery allowed to men, along with heavy silver watch chains and buckles. They took advantage of this to wear silver buttons in large numbers: at their collars and cuffs, down the front of their shirts, jackets and coats, and to fasten their breeches; breeches buttons, worn in pairs linked by an oval loop, like cuff links, could be very large (plate 62). A favourite subject for men's buttons was Joseph avoiding the unwanted attentions of Potiphar's voluptuous and half-naked wife (plate 63). These Dutch pictorial buttons enjoyed a period of great popularity in Britain at the end of the nineteenth century. As the supply of genuine old buttons was limited, many were made then, often using original stamps or casts of old buttons, specifically for export to the British market.

The round filigree buttons are a later design, appearing first in the eighteenth century (plate 64). They are usually referred to as *Zeeuwse* buttons today, but were originally worn throughout the Netherlands, not just in Zeeland, and were also found across the border in northern Germany in the late eighteenth and early nineteenth centuries.

63 **Button**
    Silver, diam. 1.7cm.
    Schoonhoven,
    Netherlands, *c.*1800.
    Private collection

    This is a man's waistcoat
    button. The design depicts
    the story of Joseph and
    Potiphar's wife (Genesis
    39.11), set in a seventeenth-
    century bedchamber, with a
    large mirror on the wall.

64 **Button (*Braamknoop*)**
    Silver filigree, diam. 2.1cm.
    Netherlands, *c.*1850.
    V&A: M.264–1925
    (Given by Miss E.J. Hipkins)

    Men's silver filigree
    braamknopen, or bramble
    buttons, are among the
    most common in the
    Netherlands. They are often
    called *Zeeuwse* buttons, as
    they are now found mainly
    in Zeeland. The coil rings
    on the front are popularly
    known as *spinnetjes*, or
    little spiders.

Central Europe

*Including Germany, Austria
and Switzerland, Poland, Hungary,
the Czech Republic and Slovakia*

At the core of central Europe is the German-speaking region of modern-day Germany, Austria and parts of Switzerland. In the past, political boundaries were constantly shifting due to dynastic alliances and the wars which ravaged the region, and this common cultural zone covered a much wider area, stretching from Poland to the northern Balkans. Although there are major differences between north and south, and between Protestant and Catholic districts, there is still more in common between the different parts than there are differences, and it makes sense to treat the traditional jewellery of this area as one unit. The former kingdom of Hungary is difficult to place, occupying an intermediate position between central and eastern Europe. Geographically and ethnically it might be expected to be part of the east, but its costume and jewellery show closer links with central Europe, evidence of its long history of a monarchy shared with Austria. Traces of the cultural influence of this central region can also be found in the jewellery of many neighbouring countries which share with it a common history.

The basic women's costume consisted of a linen or cotton blouse, a full skirt with decorative apron, and a laced bodice (plate 65). In Switzerland, Austria and Bavaria, this traditional women's costume, now called the 'Dirndl', continues to be worn on festive occasions. In Transylvania, the women of the Saxon community (plate 66) preserved some medieval German elements in their costume, including a rich marriage belt (see plate 8), and a pendant (plate 67) which had originally been a cloak clasp.

65 **Johann Friedrich Fritz,
National costume on Föhr,
1840–45**
From *Volkstümlicher
Schmuck aus
Norddeutschland*, Altonaer
Museum (Hamburg, 1979)

These women are wearing
the main distinctive items
of Föhr silver filigree
jewellery: a broad breast
chain, large buttons round
the edge of the bodice and
on the sleeves, and an apron
clasp at the back of the
waist. Traditional jewellery
continued in use on
Föhr until well into the
twentieth century.

The man's traditional costume was distinguished by a large number of buttons, sometimes accompanied by buckles, clasps and watch chains. In the lands of the old Hungarian kingdom, a distinctive official dress for men, derived from the traditional costume of the peasantry and based on a Hussar's uniform, was widely worn up to the First World War (plate 68). It was accompanied by a glittering array of jewellery, consisting of a *mente* chain (plate 69) and matching sword-belt, hat plume, and numerous buttons.

The traditional costume of the region was very tightly regulated in most places, and it is not unusual to find different pieces of jewellery worn on workdays and festivals, and in and out of mourning. In the Catholic areas in the south, religious iconography and the use of amulets play a major part. In Protestant districts, the jewellery is generally more restrained, both in style and quantity.

In the northern areas of modern-day Germany, such as the region around Hamburg, the goldsmiths who specialized in traditional jewellery mainly worked in market towns, rather than provincial capitals, and produced jewellery for the local population. This led to distinct variations in style over quite short distances. In the south, where the manufacture and distribution were arranged differently, there was much greater uniformity. Here the little town of Schwäbisch Gmünd, in southwest Germany, supplied traditional jewellery to the whole region. Schwäbisch Gmünd had become a centre for the manufacture of rosaries as early as the fifteenth century, based on outcrops of jet (a kind of fossilized coal which was

66 **Woman in festival dress, Hétfalu, Transylvania, 1910**
From *Hungarian Folk Jewellery*, T. Balogh-Horvath (Hungary, 1983)

The Saxon community in Transylvania had maintained their separate identity since they were invited to move there from Germany in the twelfth century, and their costume and rich jewellery were quite distinct from those of the host population.

67 **Pendant (*Heftel*)**
Silver-gilt set with pastes and rock crystal, diam. 13cm. M. Hanius or M. Hetzeldorfer (maker), Mediasch, Transylvania, c.1680.
V&A: M.34–1922

The *Heftel* was the most conspicuous piece of jewellery among the married women of the Saxon community in Transylvania (modern Romania). It developed from a medieval clasp (the name *Heftel* means clasp), and was worn hanging from a velvet band round the neck.

68 **Hungarian men in official dress, 1908**
Hungarian National Museum

This picture shows the son of Kossuth, the charismatic young hero of the 1848 revolution, dedicating a statue to his father on the sixtieth anniversary. He is wearing Hungarian male court dress, with a hat plume, *mente* fastener, sword belt, and masses of matching buttons.

69 *Mente* **chain**
Silver-gilt with garnets and pearls, length 51cm. Hungary, 1850–80. Private collection

The *mente* was a short coat usually worn over the shoulders with the arms hanging loose. The *mente* chain kept it from falling off. It was part of official male court dress in Hungary, but variations were worn by country people over a wider area.

easily carved) in the locality, which was used to make amulets and rosary beads. By the eighteenth century, the workshops of Schwäbisch Gmünd were making religious jewellery for the Catholic places of pilgrimage throughout the area. Later, in the mid-eighteenth century, they expanded to produce traditional jewellery of all kinds, specializing in filigree; by 1800, almost everyone in the town was involved in the industry. Mass-produced machine-made work was added in the nineteenth century. In addition to work produced in the town, similar wares were made in Austria and Switzerland, sometimes by emigrant silversmiths from Schwäbisch Gmünd. For this reason, it is often difficult to distinguish the place of manufacture for the filigree jewellery worn in southern Germany, Austria and Switzerland.

Bodice ornaments

Decorative bodice fasteners and clasps of various kinds were worn throughout the central European region, with the exception of some places in the north of Germany. In those areas, the women fastened their bodice with one large flexible clasp worn across the top (plate 71), which held down the ends of the scarf worn demurely over the open space above the neckline. In place of clasps, the edges of the bodice were decorated with large filigree buttons, which were completely non-functional (see plate 65).

Elsewhere, bodice fasteners predominated. These were mainly baroque or rococo in appearance in southern Germany, with curling hooks and scrolls. In the Cieszyn region of

70   **Pair of bodice fasteners**
     (*Hoczki*)
     Cast silver, width 4.6cm.
     Cieszyn, Silesia, Poland,
     1800–40.
     Private collection

     These bodice fasteners were
     worn in sets of up to four
     pairs at a time linked by a
     silver chain. They are larger
     and heavier than those worn
     in other parts of the region,
     and often have two, or even
     three, loops for fastening.

71 **Breast chain**
Silver filigree, width 30cm.
Föhr, north Germany,
c.1850.
V&A: 971F–1872

This elaborate breast chain
was worn by women on
the island of Föhr, off the
north coast of Germany. The
two ends were originally
a simple bodice clasp, but
over time the linking chain
became more and more
elaborate. The symbols of
an anchor, cross and heart
represent the Christian
virtues of Faith, Hope
and Charity.

Poland they were shaped like lions (plate 70) or cupids, and in Switzerland they were mainly made of filigree, with little studs at the ends. Bodice fasteners were usually made of silver, but in places such as Hungary and Slovakia they could be richly decorated with gilding, filigree, enamel and gems to match the rest of the jewellery.

The bodice fasteners were often linked by a silver chain. This had originally been a plain cord which laced the bodice tightly together, but as its decorative status became more important than its function, the two sides of the bodice slipped further and further apart, and the length of the chain increased to fill the space between. By the nineteenth century, Bavarian bodice chains were routinely up to six metres in length (plate 72). In Austria and southern Germany, the bodice tag (plate 74), which had outgrown its original function of helping to thread the chain through the fasteners, developed a large decorative head, and became a piece of jewellery worn prominently tucked into the chain. The loops of chain were further embellished with all kinds of pendants, amulets and religious medallions, of the kind worn by men on their watch chains. The whole array of bodice ornaments was probably the most important item of jewellery in the southern part of the region.

In Württemberg, in southwest Germany, and particularly in Switzerland, women wore a detachable collar over the low-cut neckline of their blouse. This was originally held in place by tapes, which were sewn to the corners and tied together under the arm. Over time, as with every other kind of fastening on traditional costume, these tapes were replaced by silver

72 **South German costume, c.1860**
From Deutsche Volkstrachten, Albert Kretschmer (Leipzig, 1865–90)

This woman from Schliersee in Bavaria is wearing a *Kropfkette* choker necklace with its decorative silver-gilt filigree clasp at the front, and a long silver bodice chain stretched between hooked fasteners. The chain is decorated with pendants, and there is a silver-gilt bodice tag tucked into the top.

73 **Collar chain (*Göllerkette*)**
Silver-gilt and silver filigree, length 89.6cm. Berne, Switzerland, 1800–70. V&A: 1325A&PART–1873

Göllerketten were worn in pairs in Switzerland to link the corners of a detachable linen collar. Like much traditional jewellery, they had long since ceased to be functional, and were purely decorative. Filigree, often partly gilded, is typical of much Swiss traditional jewellery.

74 **Bodice chain tag (*Miederstecker* or *Geschnürstift*)**
Silver, partly gilded, with filigree, blue pastes and imitation turquoise and pearl, length 13.2cm. Bavaria, south Germany, 1830–70. Private collection

The *Miederstecker* was originally used to help lace a woman's bodice. By the nineteenth century it was purely decorative and was worn tucked into the front of the bodice chain, attached by a hole in its top (here filled in).

jewellery (plate 73): ornamental chains made specifically to fulfil that function (plate 76). The chains still hung under the arm, but were much longer than the tapes they replaced, and had decorative filigree rosettes at each end, with sharp hooks to attach them to the front and back of the collar. The hook at the front often had an elaborate pendant attached as well. In Switzerland, these collar chains were sometimes accompanied by matching chains and rosettes which hung down over the apron.

Headdresses and hair ornaments

The difference between the north and south of the central European region, or perhaps more accurately the difference between Protestant and Catholic traditions, is at its greatest in the jewellery worn on the head. Married women were primarily distinguished from unmarried women by the way they wore their hair, not, as today, by the wearing of a distinctive wedding ring. The marriage ceremony was always marked by some kind

of special headdress, and married women usually celebrated their new status with a different kind of hairstyle. The sexual significance of hair, and hair pins, was particularly marked in the predominantly Catholic regions, including Bavaria, Austria and parts of Switzerland. In many areas, non-virgin brides were not allowed to wear the traditional bridal headdress, and in some places, such as Appenzell in Switzerland, a specific type of hair pin was allocated to unchaste brides.

Regardless of religious affiliation, married women usually covered their hair. In the northern Protestant regions, a bonnet or cap was sufficient. In the south, the married woman's cap was much more ornate, and women used silver hair pins to hold it in place. These hair pins came in a wide variety of shapes and sizes, appropriate to the different ways in which they were worn in different places. In Bavaria, married women wore a decorative cap, extravagantly embroidered all over with gold thread; small double-pronged hair pins with silver filigree heads were inserted round the rim to hold it in place. In contrast, younger unmarried women wore a single larger pin, skewered through a kind of doughnut enclosing their bunched hair. In Catholic central Switzerland and Appenzell, the hair pins were larger still, up to 30cm in length, and decorated with filigree, enamel and glass pastes (plate 75). They were worn horizontally at the back of the head, stuck through their owner's long braided hair (plate 76).

Earrings were not an important part of the traditional costume. They rarely appeared before the nineteenth century, and then mainly in Catholic districts. Women in the few

75 **Hair pin**
Silver, partly gilded, with silver filigree set with red pastes and enamel, length 16.7cm. F.L. Beul (maker), Lachen, central Switzerland, 1800–70.
V&A: 102–1872

―――――――――――

This hair pin was worn by young women, at the back of the head, stuck through their braided hair. It may have been cut down, because it is shorter than is usual. These hair pins reached their largest size around 1900. It would have been kept in its own carved wooden box.

76 **Ludwig Vogel, Illustration of a young woman from Beckenried, central Switzerland, 1814**
From 'Peasant art in Switzerland', *The Studio* (London, 1924)

―――――――――――

This woman is wearing a large hair pin on the back of her head, a choker necklace round her neck, and silver chains under her arms and across her bodice. The direction of the hair pin, from right to left, shows that she is unmarried.

Protestant areas that adopted earrings into their traditional costume, such as Lindhorst in Lower Saxony, usually hooked them into their headdress, rather than their ears, as in the Netherlands.

Necklaces and chains

Necklaces were worn throughout the region. In many places, they took the form of chokers, made of embroidered cloth sometimes appliquéd with silver plaques in the north, and rows of beads or silver chains with fancy clasps in the south. In Hungary, the chains were made of decorative rosettes, and in Switzerland of filigree plaques, linked by garnet-coloured beads (plate 77). The German name for the chain chokers worn in Austria and Bavaria, *Kropfketten* (goitre chains) (plate 78), reveals their purpose: they were intended to conceal the ugly swelling of the throat caused by goitre, a disease of iodine deficiency, which was endemic in the Alpine region before the twentieth century. Long after improvements in modern medicine eliminated the disease, these necklaces remain in common use today for festive events. Their decorative clasps are usually worn at the front of the neck (plate 72), although portraits show that they originally started at the nape, and

gradually worked their way round to the front over time, as they became larger and more imposing.

Chokers were not the only kind of necklace found in the south German region. Before the *Kropfkette* became dominant, women tied a light gauze scarf of black silk round their necks. By the end of the eighteenth century this had acquired a decorative clasp (see plate 4), which grew in size and complexity throughout the nineteenth century until it became so unwieldy that it was often left hanging down unfastened. Around Nuremberg, women wore a delicate necklace of filigree plaques interspersed with cut gemstones (see plate 14). The design clearly derives from court dress of the eighteenth century, but it acquired a specific two-tiered design in that region, and continued in use there long after it had gone out of fashion elsewhere.

Bead necklaces were worn in many places, usually with decorative silver clasps. In the north, amber from the Baltic was the most popular material, lightly worked to preserve the size of the individual beads as much as possible. In Germany, amber necklaces were most common inland, but in Poland they were concentrated in the Baltic coastal region. Elsewhere, Polish women preferred necklaces made of coral. The Swiss also used coral beads in their chokers in the eighteenth century, but had

77 **Necklace (*Halsbätti*)**
Silver-gilt filigree with garnet-coloured glass beads, length 34.5cm. Canton of Schwyz, Switzerland, 1800–70.
V&A: 161–1870

The name *Halsbätti* means a neck rosary, but this necklace had no religious significance. It simply refers to the beads, usually made of facetted glass imitating garnet, of the kind also used in rosaries. It was worn over a band of black gauze.

78 **Necklace (*Kropfkette*)**
Silver filigree with garnets and imitation pearl, length 32cm. Austria, 1840–70.
V&A: M.430–1911
(Given by Jane Souter Hipkins)

The *Kropfkette* (goitre chain) was originally worn to hide the neck swelling caused by goitre. The snap clasp at the front has snaps on both sides, so that it can be used interchangeably with other necklaces.

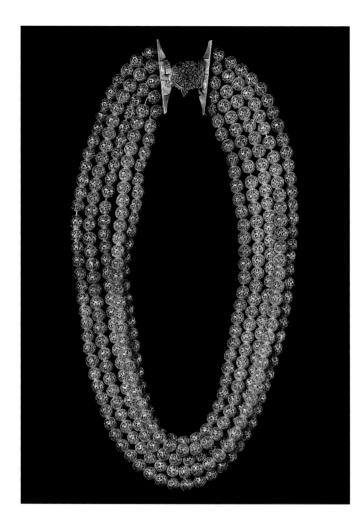

mainly switched to garnet, or, more often, garnet-coloured glass, by the mid-nineteenth century (plate 77). Garnet necklaces were also popular in neighbouring Swabia. These garnet beads were usually facetted rather than smooth, as facetted beads would reflect more light in the candle-lit rooms of the time, but they also often had an amuletic purpose, helping to deflect evil of all kinds. The women of the Altes Land (plate 79), near Hamburg, wore long, multi-tiered necklaces of hollow silver or silver filigree beads (plate 80). It was only in Poland, in the east of the region, and the lands of the Hungarian kingdom, that necklaces of glass beads, usually of multiple strands, were worn in any quantity from choice.

Brooches

Medieval-style ring brooches (see Chapter 1) formed part of the women's costume only in the north. In the Vierlande, near Hamburg, women wore plain, flat engraved circles on weekdays, and richer gilded ones, decorated with filigree, enamel and coloured pastes, on Sundays and festivals (plate 82). In the neighbouring Altes Land, women's brooches were heart-shaped (plate 81). Elsewhere, ring brooches were mainly worn by men. These were heart-shaped in a broad band across the south, from Alsace in France, through southern Germany and northern Switzerland to Austria (see plate 6). They were often gifts of love, as can be seen from the dates and inscriptions frequently found on them. Well into the twentieth century, men in Poland and Slovakia continued to wear heart-shaped ring brooches made of brass and often fitted with separate tangs attached by

79 **Women in Altes Land costume**

From *Deutsche Volkstrachten*, A. Kretschmer (Leipzig, 1865–90)

These women in their traditional Sunday church-going costume are wearing all the appropriate silver filigree jewellery of the Altes Land, near Hamburg, including a multi-strand necklace of silver beads with a decorative clasp at the back, a heart-shaped brooch, spherical buttons on the sleeves, and large shoe buckles.

80 **Necklace**

Silver filigree beads with a silver-gilt filigree clasp set with imitation turquoise and garnet pastes, length 88cm. Altes Land, near Hamburg, Germany, *c*.1888. V&A: 519–1899

This necklace was worn over the outer clothes on Sundays and festivals. It has its owner's name and a date engraved on the back of the clasp, suggesting that it was probably a betrothal gift.

short lengths of chain. Brooches with spring catches, of the kind familiar in fashionable dress in Europe from the late seventeenth century onwards, rarely form part of traditional costume anywhere, but do appear in some areas, including Switzerland and Croatia, in the late nineteenth century.

Amulets, rosaries and other religious jewellery

Religious jewellery and amulets of all kinds were worn only in Catholic areas. Although the Catholic Church disapproved of the wearing of amulets, considering the practice idolatrous and unChristian, it was powerless to prevent it; traditional beliefs were too deeply engrained in the minds of the inhabitants of the Alpine region, who would have been largely unaware of any conflict. They hung amulets made from patterned stones (plate 84) or animal parts side by side with religious reliquaries (plate 85) and medallions on their rosaries, bodice chains and watch chains (plate 86). However, the identification of amulets with Catholic belief was strong enough almost to eliminate their visible use in Protestant parts of the region, although secret beliefs inevitably survived in many places.

In the Catholic south, many new pilgrimage sites, often dedicated to the Virgin Mary, sprang up in the late seventeenth century, offering souvenirs supplied by the silversmiths of Schwäbisch Gmünd. These rosaries, medallions, rings, etc, each with the attributes of the appropriate patron, were bought in enormous numbers by pilgrims to attract the benevolence of the saint, and to protect against evil. Rosaries were an essential part of the jewellery worn by church-going women on Sundays.

81 **Heart-shaped ring brooch (Bruthart)**
Silver filigree set with imitation turquoise and garnet, length 7.7cm. Altes Land, near Hamburg, Germany, c.1864.
V&A: 530–1899

This heart-shaped ring brooch was worn by women at the neck to close their blouse (see plate 79). It was probably a love gift, as it has its original owner's name and the date '1864' engraved on the back. Turquoises stand for friendship, and garnets for love.

82 **Ring brooch (Hemdspange)**
Silver-gilt filigree with red pastes, diam. 7.2cm. Vierlande, Hamburg, Germany, 1800–70.
V&A: 527–1899

Women wore ring brooches in only a few areas of Germany. This ring brooch was used on Sundays and festivals by women in the Vierlande. On other days they wore a plain silver ring brooch with engraved decoration.

They were made of beads carved from amuletic materials, such as mother-of-pearl or terebinth wood from the Holy Land, coral, rock crystal or agate and were carried in the hand with the service book, whose filigree fittings matched the paternoster beads of the rosary.

Coins were also used as pendants, particularly those portraying the Virgin Mary, and they often played an important part in marriage and christening ceremonies. They were sometimes carefully mounted in elaborate frames, or hung from complex arrangements of chains, which could cover the entire front of the bodice. The Catholic women of Lucerne, in central Switzerland, wore gilded pendants set with religious images painted on glass or enamel (plate 83). Another popular amulet, particularly for soldiers and travellers, was the *Georgsthaler*, based on a Mansfeld coin of the seventeenth century, which showed St George killing the dragon. The original coin had providentially saved a German officer's life by deflecting a French bullet, and it consequently became immensely popular as a talisman against sudden or violent death.

Rings

In the deeply conservative world of German traditional costume, rings were never worn purely for decoration. They fulfilled a number of specific purposes, and often several at the same time. Betrothal rings were used throughout the region. The betrothal was a binding commitment, often considered more important than the wedding ceremony itself, and the main symbol of

84 **Amulet (***Krätzenstein***)**
Fossilized coral set in silver, length 3.4cm. Traunstein, Bavaria, Germany, c.1800.
V&A: M.26–1917
(Given by Dr W.L. Hildburgh)

Fossilized coral was found in the Alpine region. It was often made into amulets, usually heart-shaped, as it was believed to be highly effective against witches. The Italian name for fossilized coral is *pietra stregonia* (witches stone).

85 **Amulet**
Silver filigree with glass and wax, length 4.1cm. Schwäbisch Gmünd, south Germany, 1830–50.
V&A: M.36–1917
(Given by Dr W.L. Hildburgh)

This amulet represents the tongue of St John Nepomuk, which was reportedly found uncorrupted when his tomb at Prague was opened in 1719. The amulet was believed to protect against malicious rumours and lies.

86 **Amulets (***Walburgisbüchse***,** ***Schneckendeckel*** **and** ***Neidfeige***)**
Silver filigree, operculum shell and bone, length 5.6cm. South Germany, 1750–1800.
V&A: 909–1872

Amulets and religious pendants were often worn side by side. The filigree case has the initials of St Walburga on its side, and would have contained a phial of liquid from her tomb. The operculum shell was worn to promote fertility and to help in childbirth, and the bone fist to protect against the evil eye.

83 **Pendant (***Trachtendeli***)**
Silver-gilt with filigree, enamel and reverse-painted glass, length 10.5cm. Lucerne, Switzerland, c.1800.
V&A: 163–1872

A *Trachtendeli* is a pendant worn by Catholic women in the central part of Switzerland. The name derives from the French word *médaille* (medallion). Sometimes there is a religious image on one side, and a romantic image on the other, so that the wearer could reverse it for appropriate occasions.

this contract was a ring. In Bavaria, a betrothal ring was one of the earliest pieces of jewellery allowed to peasants in the seventeenth century. In a few places, betrothal rings were made of gold, but silver, or silver-gilt, rings were much more common, and the poor made do with tin or brass. These rings were often decorated with appropriate symbols, such as hearts, flowers or clasped hands, and set with coloured pastes (plate 87). Red was recognized as the colour of love, and green of hope. Wedding rings, in comparison, were much less significant. Unlike the ubiquitous plain gold ring used today, there was no universal pattern, and women felt no need to wear them at all times.

In predominantly Catholic areas, rings were expected to play their part in protecting the wearer from the random dangers of daily life. Many carried the symbols or images of saints, or members of the Holy Family (plate 88), and were bought as souvenirs at places of pilgrimage. Others were set with objects which had amuletic qualities, such as crystal, stag's teeth (see plate 3), or shells. A great number of the rings worn in south Germany were made in Schwäbisch Gmünd. The size and weight of some of the rings worn by men suggest that they were intended to act as knuckledusters, providing physical, rather than spiritual, protection (plate 89).

Belts, buckles and clasps

Before the general adoption of wedding rings, belts were the main item of jewellery used to indicate a woman's married status. These were late medieval in origin, and wedding belts still survived in a number of places in the region in the

87 Ring
Silver filigree with reverse-painted glass over red foil, and red pastes, diam. 2.8cm. Schwäbisch Gmünd, south Germany, 1800–40. V&A: 911–1872

The glass bezel, showing a naïve gilt image of a flower, is an example of the *verre eglomisé* work which was one of the specialities of southern Germany. These rings can have religious motifs, or symbols of love. The flower suggests it was a betrothal gift.

88 Ring
Silver, partly gilded, set with red pastes, diam. 2.9cm. Schwäbisch Gmünd, south Germany, 1800–50. V&A: 979–1871

This ring has the image of the Madonna of Neukirchen beim Heiligen Blut, although the design of the ring can also be found with other religious images in the centre. Schwäbisch Gmünd produced souvenirs for many pilgrimage sites in the south German region.

89 Ring
Cast brass, diam. 3.7cm. Bavaria, Germany, 1800–70. V&A: 916–1872

Rings could have physical as well as symbolic uses. This ring was described as 'used as a weapon by peasant lads in Upper Bavaria', when it was acquired by the V&A in 1872.

nineteenth century, including Schwalm, in German Hesse, the Austrian province of Carniola (now Slovenia), Poland, and most conspicuously among the Saxon community of Transylvania (see plate 8). South German marriage belts, sometimes converted into more useful necklaces, became a popular souvenir for British tourists (see plate 13). However, most women only wore a metal clasp on a cloth or leather belt, and, as a relative newcomer, the clasp had little significance in the traditional costume.

Silver buckles, fastened by a prong rather than a hook, were mainly worn on shoes, following the aristocratic fashion of the seventeenth and eighteenth centuries. They were used by both men and women with their church-going costume on Sundays, and at other festive events; both the shoes and the buckles were far too expensive for everyday use. In southwest Germany, men wore hat buckles, which had long ceased to secure the ribbon round the brim of their hat and were purely decorative. Ornate clasps and fittings fastened their church-going books on Sundays; bibles in the north, and service books in the south.

Buttons

The silver buttons of the central zone are among the most diverse in Europe. In the western parts of the region, men's costumes, based on urban fashions of the seventeenth century, included buttons in large numbers, which were worn equally by Catholics and Protestants. Hungarian male costume always included buttons, worn on a long sleeveless waistcoat, and on the jackets and coats traditionally worn slung over the shoulder (see plate 68). In some areas, women's costume, and even that of children, included buttons.

Hungarian buttons are usually cone-shaped or oval, of the kind worn further east, in Russia. They remained an important element of Hungarian dress, particularly among herdsmen and gypsies as well as at court, up to the beginning of the twentieth century. The most impressive were worn by men, and were employed as an indication of rank and identity. Elsewhere, round or domed filigree buttons are the commonest type, either made entirely of filigree, or with an open filigree front and a sheet silver back. In the north of the German-speaking region, the filigree technique is much more structured than in the south, where the filigree patterns used by the goldsmiths of Schwäbisch Gmünd are looser and less clearly defined. Because of the labour involved, filigree buttons were always more expensive than those made entirely of sheet silver. In the Altes Land, near Hamburg, the large filigree buttons worn by women (plate 90) were considered too ostentatious to be appropriate wear during mourning, when they were replaced by half filigree, or sheet silver buttons. In contrast, many of the earlier buttons from Bavaria and Upper Austria were made of silver-plated brass or copper, reflecting the relative poverty of the rural population there in the second half of the eighteenth century. Along the Danube, among the expatriate German communities in Hungary and Slovakia, elegant filigree buttons were often preserved as heirlooms over many generations.

90   **Button**
Silver filigree, diam. 2.5cm.
Altes Land, near Hamburg,
Germany, 1800–70.
V&A: 526–1899

This button would have been worn by a woman, as part of a set of twelve, on the seams of her sleeves. The little applied triangles, between the discs, which form a starfish pattern, are typical of buttons from the Altes Land.

France

It is harder to identify the roots of traditional jewellery in France than in any other country in Europe, as there is very little evidence of any kind much earlier than the mid-eighteenth century. Yet the jewellery that appeared at the end of the eighteenth century, as if from nowhere, is so distinctive, not only in its design but even in the way that it is worn, that it must have had deep and tenacious roots in French rural life (plate 91).

The way that jewellery was made and sold in France also differed. A far higher proportion of French traditional jewellery was mass-produced than in other countries, using stamping in matrices for example, and this was associated with the concentration of the industry in large centres. As early as the beginning of the nineteenth century, much traditional jewellery was made in Paris, rather than locally. This jewellery was then exported wholesale to the region, where it was finished off, assembled and sold by local retailers, or distributed to itinerant peddlers for sale at large annual fairs, or those which sprang up at the numerous pilgrimage sites on their patronal feast days. Perhaps because of this early mass-production, the French traditional jewellery which survives is more likely to be made of base metal, usually plated with gold or silver, than it is elsewhere.

Only a few areas of France, mainly those with strong local identities such as Normandy or Brittany, have any distinctive traditional jewellery. Most French jewellery worn in the nineteenth century, in particular the earrings, is indistinguishable from the fashionable jewellery worn

91 **Woman in dress of Bourg-Saint-Maurice, Savoy, France**
From *Costumes, Traditions and Songs of Savoy*, Estella Canziani (London, 1911)

This woman is wearing a pair of gold crescent earrings, and a gold *croix Jeannette*. The cross is worn in the French way, with a heart-shaped *coulant*, but on a gold chain rather than a black velvet ribbon. Use of a chain, which was probably Italian in origin, was common in Savoy.

4

throughout Europe at the time, and details of costume, particularly the lace headdress, were the most important means of regional identification. Even so, French traditional jewellery is quite different from that worn in other countries in Europe, and clearly identifiable. But a new kind of regional jewellery developed alongside the traditional jewellery, partly to augment its important role in economic tourism, but also possibly to express the concepts of regional identity which would have been embodied in the original jewellery which no longer existed, yet which survived undisturbed in most other countries. Examples include Bressan enamels (see plate 104), and the Celtic silver jewellery of Brittany. For these reasons, the landscape of French traditional jewellery is quite different from that of other countries.

Crosses and other religious pendants

As elsewhere in Catholic Europe, the cross was the most distinctive piece of jewellery (plate 92). The most characteristic French cross, found throughout the country, and in neighbouring regions as far away as Dalmatia, is a hollow stamped cross with trefoil ends called a *croix Jeannette* (plate 93). The name confirms its widespread use; it derives from the practice of hiring servant girls on St John's day, the 24th of June, who promptly bought a cross with their first earnings. These 'simple' crosses are often made of gilt metal, rather than gold, as suited the modest means of their buyers, but there is nothing simple about either their appearance or manufacture. They are richly decorated in the centre and at

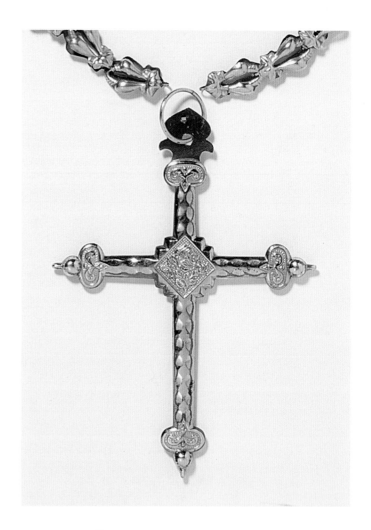

92   **Cross pendant**
      (*Croix boulonnaise* or *Croix de pardon*)
      Silver filigree, length 5.7cm.
      Boulogne-sur-Mer, France,
      1850–1900.
      Private collection

      The *croix boulonnaise* was worn by the women of the fishing community of Boulogne. Their jewellery often features marine symbols, such as scallop shells. The filigree design may date from the time of Spanish occupation in the sixteenth and seventeenth centuries.

93   **Cross pendant**
      (*Croix Jeannette*)
      Stamped gilded metal,
      length 11.9cm.
      V. Poissant (maker),
      Paris, France, *c*.1860.
      V&A: 324:2–1868

      The *croix Jeannette*, meaning St John's cross, was the most widespread type of cross in France, and was usually worn on a black velvet ribbon. The name derives from the custom for servant girls to buy them on their first pay day, St John's day.

the ends of the arms with symbolic motifs such as pansies or religious symbols, and can be up to 10cm in length. The decoration was stamped on the thin sheet metal by steel dies.

Although crosses are found in all Catholic countries, the way that they are worn in France is different. They are normally hung on a length of black velvet ribbon, accompanied by a slide called a *coulant*. The *coulant*, usually heart-shaped, has a decorative front, with three holes, rings or bars on the back. The wearer threaded the ribbon through the holes, so that a loop of ribbon hung down at the front to support the cross. The ribbon was then fastened round the neck like a choker, with the ends tied at the back in a bow, and with the cross hanging down vertically at the front, separated by some centimetres from the *coulant*.

The largest and most decorative of French crosses come from Normandy. The *croix bosse* (plate 94), made from stamped bosses arranged to create a large hollow cross with the lowest arm hanging loose at the bottom, is one of the earliest and most widespread designs. Most of the other Normandy crosses are set with imitation diamonds of glass or local rock crystal (plate 95). The rock crystals originally came from Alençon in Lower Normandy, but by the nineteenth century the quarries were exhausted and most '*diamants d'Alençon*' were imported from Savoy or the Pyrenees. Similar crosses are found across the border in Belgium. Another Normandy cross, gold set with rock crystal, is the *croix de Rouen* (plate 96). Traditional crosses also survived in Provence and Savoy. The most distinctive type in Savoy was

94 **Cross pendant (*Croix bosse*) and slide (*Coulant*)**
Stamped gold with applied filigree, length 15.5cm. Paris, France, 1798–1809. V&A: 59–1869

The *croix bosse*, so called due to the stamped bosses which make up the cross, is the most common Normandy cross. These crosses are usually made of gold, silver-gilt or gilded metal. The accompanying heart-shaped slide is always made of thin sheet metal with a filigree overlay.

an austere equilateral cross with flared, often pierced, ends, but the most characteristic feature of Savoyard crosses was the use of a stylized bow instead of a *coulant* (see Chapter 5).

In Brittany, the cross was worn without a *coulant* (see plate 12). A pendent strip of black velvet ribbon was sewn to the centre of the velvet choker, and the cross was attached to its end. Because the width of the strip at the front was not restricted by being threaded through the *coulant*, it could be decorated with spangles and sequins, and these were also sprinkled along the front and ends of the ribbon. When the French commissioners of the International Exhibition held in London in 1872 were asked for examples of traditional French jewellery, necklaces such as these were among the pieces they provided. Afterwards they were put on display at the South Kensington Museum. 'Breton necklets', as they were called at the time, were greatly admired and for a short period became immensely fashionable in Britain.

Pendants in the shape of a dove, the symbol of the Holy Spirit, were worn in northern France and the Auvergne. The Normandy dove is completely covered with clear pastes or crystals, and holds a branch set with coloured stones in its beak (plate 97). An earlier and simpler version (plate 98) had three small pendants hanging from the lower edge, representing the wounds of Christ. This is very similar to the *Saint-Esprit* which survived in the Auvergne. The same arrangement of three pendants can also be found on pendent crosses (plate 99).

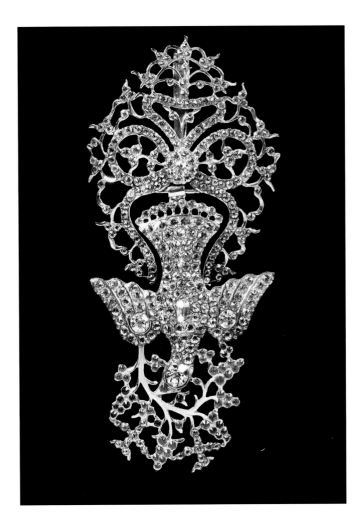

95 **Cross pendant (*Croix de Saint-Lô*) and slide (*Coulant*)**
Silver set with rock crystal, length 16cm. Normandy, France, 1809–19.
V&A: 70–1869

The *croix de Saint-Lô* is named for the town where it was worn most. It is also sometimes called *a croix quadrille*, due to its lozenge shape. It was the first of the Normandy crosses to be set with stones – usually rock crystals, which are native to Normandy.

96 **Cross pendant (*Croix de Rouen*) and slide (*Coulant*)**
Gold set with rock crystal and pastes, length 10.4cm. Normandy, France, 1798–1809.
V&A: 63–1869

The *croix de Rouen*, named after the town where it was worn, is one of the largest and latest of the Normandy crosses. It was always made of gold-coloured metal, set with rock crystals, and probably derives from the *croix de Saint-Lô*.

97 **Pendant (*Saint-Esprit*)**
Gold set with pastes, length 12.7cm. Normandy, France, 1798–1809.
V&A: 264–1869

The *Saint-Esprit* pendant represents the Holy Spirit in the form of a dove. This version, with a sprig of grapevine in its beak, picked out in coloured pastes, is typical of Normandy. It also signified marriage and fertility.

Clasps

Not every woman in Normandy was rich enough to wear a fine gold cross, but almost everyone could afford a silver clasp, or *agrafe*, for her cloak. These were worn universally, by all levels of society, from the late eighteenth until well into the twentieth century (plate 100). The most characteristic are made of stamped silver, facetted in imitation of the aristocratic cut-steel jewellery of the eighteenth century, but, like most traditional jewellery, they soon developed their own distinctive appearance. The earliest are small and practical, but over the course of the nineteenth century they increased in size and many are over 15cm wide. Similar clasps were worn in the Poitou region, and probably other parts of France. They were also found in the Netherlands in the nineteenth century, where they may have been introduced during the Napoleonic occupation. Men's silver clasps are much heavier and stronger (although smaller) than women's clasps. As with other functional jewellery, such as belt hooks and buttons, French traditional clasps are made of silver rather than gold.

Necklaces

The *esclavage*, a magnificent creation of gold chains and plaques, was the most important traditional necklace in France (plate 101). It was primarily a marriage piece, as its name implies, and was an important part of the dowry. The constituent chains could cost up to 1,000 francs each in the nineteenth century – the price of two good cows – yet it had the great advantage that it could be enhanced over time, and

98 **Pendant (*Saint-Esprit*)**
Silver, length 5.2cm.
P-A. Dachery (maker),
Amiens, France, 1766–75.
Private collection

The *Saint-Esprit* pendant was worn in many regions of France, by Protestants as well as Catholics. The three pendants represent the wounds of Christ, and are found on many traditional French crosses and religious pendants.

99 **Cross reliquary**
Silver, length 5cm.
France, 1798–1809.
Private collection.

This cross is typical of those worn in Brittany, although it was probably made in Paris. It has Christ on one side, under the title INRI, and Mary, under a canopy, on the other. The back is hinged and permanently fastened with a pin.

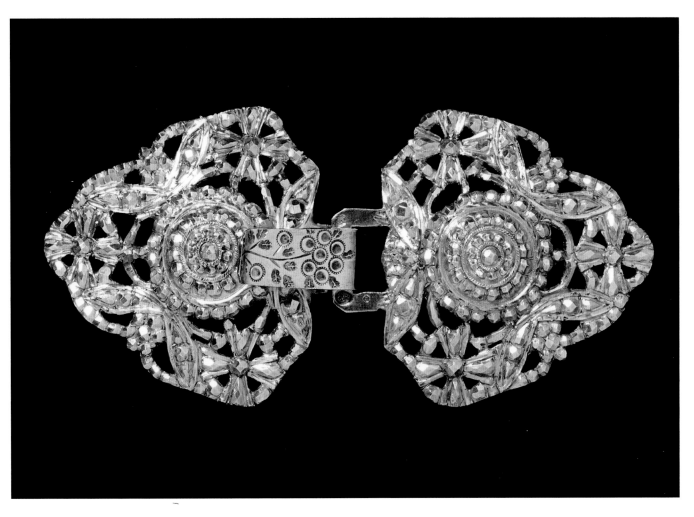

100 **Clasp (*Agrafe*)**
Stamped silver, width
13.6cm. Normandy, France,
1809–19.
V&A: 91&A–1869

The *agrafe*, or cloak clasp,
is the most typical item of
Normandy jewellery. All but
the poorest women would
have owned one in the
nineteenth century.
They are always made
of silver sheet, which is
pierced and stamped to
imitate cut-steel.

101 **Necklace (*Esclavage*)**
Normandy, France,
1800–1900. From *Bijoux des
regions de France*, Claudette
Joannis (Paris, 1992)

The *esclavage*, meaning
slavery or chains, was
the most expensive type
of traditional necklace in
France. It was typically a
marriage gift, but could be
enriched with more chains
throughout the owner's
life. The decoration of the
plaques varies by region.

extra chains were often added at the birth of a child, or with an increase in prosperity. The *esclavage* was worn in the same way in most places, with only the plaques sometimes varying by region.

There are few other distinctive necklaces. The *collier d'Yvetot*, from Normandy, consisted of a narrow row of small units set with clear pastes, with a matching strip supporting a cross or *Saint-Esprit* hanging down at the front, but although this necklace was only worn in Normandy, most were made in Paris. Women in Provence had a rich necklace of diamonds set in gold, which matched the local cross.

Brooches

As in other European countries, the only brooches worn with traditional costume were ring brooches (see Chapter 1). These were worn by men, mainly in western France, to fasten their shirts at the neck, or to hold a cravat neatly in place. Women used small pins with decorative faces, like stick pins or modern brooches, to fasten their shawls and caps. Some of the men's brooches are plain circles, but most are heart-shaped, often decorated with symbols, such as hearts or arrows which may indicate that they were betrothal gifts, or emblems of their owner's profession such as tools or cows. In the Vendée, where resistance to the French Revolution was strongest, a double heart was adopted as a patriotic symbol of adherence to the old regime, and it is still commonly worn today, although now more often as a tie pin or modern brooch, with a spring fitting on the back (plate 102). French ring brooches, both

102 **Brooch (*Coeur vendéen*)**
Silver, length 5.3cm.
E. Loze (maker), Niort,
France, 1849–77.
Private collection

The *coeur vendéen* is descended from a medieval ring brooch, and has clear links to the Scottish luckenbooth brooch. During the French Revolution it became a symbol of Royalist and Catholic resistance. It has remained a popular souvenir in the region to this day.

round and heart-shaped, may have crossed the Atlantic in the eighteenth century. The ring brooches used in the fur trade in North America (see plate 9) are usually attributed to Scottish influence, but the French involvement in trade and silver-working at the time was so strong that an early French contribution seems credible.

Belt hooks

Perhaps because of their practical nature, belt hooks survived as part of traditional costume in many regions of France, where more decorative pieces of jewellery vanished entirely. They are made of sturdy silver, with a single loop at the front holding a large S-shaped hook for the chain (plate 103). They were mainly used to hold a pair of scissors or a knife – essential tools for the sewing, embroidery or lace-making which were an important part of many women's lives. Like most traditional jewellery in France, they were part of the dowry, to such an extent that the wearing of a belt hook was often considered one of the identifying marks of a married woman. The belt hook differs from the fashionable chatelaine in having only one pendant, whereas the chatelaine has numerous hooks.

Bressan enamels

The town of Bourg-en-Bresse, in the southeast near Lyon, is famous for its enamels. These are made as tiny plaques, decorated with paillettes of gold and set with stones or glass pastes, which are then mounted in jewellery as if they were gems themselves (plate 104). The origins of the industry are

103 **Belt hook** (*Crochet*)
Silver, length 10.7cm.
J-A. Minoret (maker), Niort, France, 1826–38.
Private collection

The *crochet* was the symbol of a married woman, and was used throughout France. It was worn tucked into her belt, with a long double chain, which usually held a pair of scissors, attached to the hole at the base. This design with a heart is typical of the region of Poitou.

unknown. Although there are records of enamel workers at Bourg in the Middle Ages, the earliest surviving pieces of this kind of work are from around 1850, and the industry was at its peak in the second half of the nineteenth century. It is unlikely that there was ever any distinctive traditional jewellery based on these enamels, although the women of Bourg were happy to wear them with their traditional costume, and there are many prints from the late nineteenth century showing this fashion. However, Bressan enamels were among the pieces of 'traditional' jewellery chosen for the London International Exhibition of 1872, and helped to establish the image of natural French artistic taste among the British.

104 **Cross pendant**
Silver-gilt filigree set with Bressan enamels and red and green pastes, length 8.4cm. Paul Ydot (maker), Paris, France, c.1870.
V&A: 1228–1873

The enamels on this cross come from Bourg-en-Bresse. They were not fired directly onto the metal, but made individually and then set like gems. Many were exported and used by jewellers outside the region. This cross was made by Paul Ydot of Paris, who specialized in making such jewellery.

Italy

In many respects, the traditional jewellery of Italy is very similar to that of its Catholic neighbours. Large areas of southern Italy were under Spanish rule until 1713, and many places in northern Italy were under foreign administration at various times up to the mid-nineteenth century, mainly by France and the Austrian Empire. It was not until 1861 that Italy finally achieved a degree of unification. Despite this fractured political background, the cultural heritage is more unified, and there are aspects of the traditional costume and jewellery which are quite distinct. Ticino in Switzerland, Malta, and some parts of the Adriatic coast also belong in this region, as far as their material culture is concerned.

Women's traditional costume in nineteenth-century Italy, consisting of a laced bodice, with or without (often detachable) sleeves, a full skirt, shift and jacket, with head scarves and aprons in various places, was still essentially a seventeenth-century dress. The jewellery mainly derives from the same era. Earrings and crosses were the most important items, often based on forms popular in aristocratic jewellery of the seventeenth and eighteenth centuries. Women secured their hair with decorative hair pins (plate 105) and hung rosaries of expensive materials or manufacture round their necks and wrists. Both men and women wore rings, which were sometimes betrothal gifts; wedding rings were a very late addition to the *corredo*, the set of jewellery considered appropriate to a married woman. The main piece used to signify marriage was traditionally a wedding belt, but this had fallen out of use everywhere by the nineteenth century, except

105   **Jean Portaels, portrait of Charlotte, wife of the Archduke Maximilian,**
Milan, 1857
Miramare Castle,
Trieste, Italy
©/Lebrecht Music & Arts

Princess Charlotte of Belgium married the Hapsburg Archduke Maximilian in Milan in 1857, at the age of seventeen. This painting shows her wearing the traditional *raggiera* headdress of the Brianza region of Lombardy, the region around Milan. The *raggiera* was also celebrated by Alessandro Manzoni in his 1827 novel *I promessi sposi*.

5

in the village of Piana dei Greci (now Piana degli Albanesi) in Sicily, where women wore a magnificent heavy silver marriage belt (plate 106).

Wherever possible, Italian women wore gold, even if it was rolled as thin as paper (plate 107). In the north, the metal used was usually of high carat yellow gold, while in the south they tended to prefer a warmer red gold, often of lower standard, and sometimes mixed with yellow gold filigree inserts (plate 108). Silver was usually reserved for more functional items, such as hair pins, clasps and amulets. Where colours were used, red predominated; many pieces were worn with crimson ribbons, and the most popular stones were garnets, red pastes and coral.

Although the colour was important, Italians had a clear preference for real gems, and if they could not afford them they went to considerable lengths to use imitations that

106 **Marriage belt (*Brezi*)**
Cast silver, partly gilded, length 63.6cm (belt) and width 13cm (clasp). P.C. and A.M.(makers), Palermo, Italy, 1710 (belt) and
c. 1750 (clasp).
V&A: M.65:1&2–1949
(Given by Mrs E.M. Richards)

This belt comes from the village of Piana degli Albanesi, in Sicily. It was worn by married women of the community which fled there from Albania in the fifteenth century to escape the Ottoman Turks. The figure of St George on the clasp represents their patron saint.

107 Necklace
Hollow gold beads with
applied filigree, on red silk,
length 42cm. Lombardy,
Italy, 1820–60.
V&A: 385–1868

The gold of these beads
is paper thin, and many
are dented from use. The
applied filigree decoration is
typical of jewellery from the
region. It became known as
Etruscan work in Britain in
the later nineteenth century.

were as close to the natural stone as possible. As early as the
sixteenth century, Benvenuto Cellini, the famous goldsmith,
records the use of doublets in peasant jewellery. These tiny
slivers of real gem, mounted on glass to give the illusion of
a larger, finer stone, are equally common in nineteenth-century
Italian traditional jewellery. Metal foils were used as backing for
glass pastes and low-quality stones to improve their appearance.
Pearls were popular throughout the region. They were pierced
and set as gems in the north (plate 109), and sewn in swathes
to the surface of the piece, as beads threaded on very fine gold
wire, in the south. In more remote places, such as Sardinia and
parts of the Abruzzo region, an older tradition survived. Here
the jewellery was often made of silver, from choice rather than
necessity, and preserved medieval forms and motifs.

Men had little traditional jewellery, except in the former
Spanish-ruled regions, where they wore silver toggle buttons.
Throughout Italy, but particularly in the south, men, women and
children used numerous amulets and religious pendants.

Although most jewellery was acquired at marriage, as
everywhere in Europe, traditional jewellery was also handed
down from generation to generation in the female line,
to nieces if there were no daughters. Where there were
several potential inheritors, custom sometimes decreed
that the bequest should be split equally, which led to the
destruction of sets or even individual pieces. It is rare to find
complete Venetian or Maltese chains, as these were often
chopped into equal parts to fulfil the requirements of these
inheritance customs.

Earrings

Earrings are the most common type of traditional jewellery throughout Italy; Italian women had their ears pierced almost at birth, and wore earrings throughout their lives. The range of designs reflects the various cultural influences in the region. Many have a relatively simple top, consisting of a decorative front attached to a hinged wire, with a much larger, and even more decorative, pendant (plate 110). The pendant was often hooked loosely onto the wire, so that it could be removed easily while the woman was working, and reattached for Sundays or festivals. This method of attachment had the advantage of allowing the owner to create a number of jewels from a limited range of parts; it is not uncommon to find pairs of earrings whose pendants are quite different from their tops. These pendent earrings are usually derived from seventeenth- and eighteenth-century designs for aristocratic jewellery. The *girandole*, which first appeared in court jewellery in the seventeenth century, has three drops hanging from a central plaque, often via a stylized bow (plate 111).

Other types of earring have an older heritage. The stylized vase, found laden with pearls in the area around Venice (plate 113), and in some of the Greek islands, derives ultimately from classical Greek or Roman prototypes. In the south, women wore hoop earrings, consisting, at their simplest, of a ring of wire threaded through the lobe of the ear. The majority were much larger and more elaborate (plate 112); those with the lower edge swollen to a hollow crescent shape were called *navicella*, as they resembled ships (plate 114). The crescent shape may be

108 **Pendent earring**
Yellow gold filigree with red gold facings, length 9.3cm. Antonio Caccavallo (maker), Naples, Italy, 1832–67.
V&A: 301–1868

The mix of yellow gold filigree and red sheet gold in this earring is typical of southern Italian traditional jewellery. It was made by Antonio Caccavallo of Naples, but was worn in Sardinia.

109 **Earring**
Gold set with pearls, length 7.9cm. Tuscany, Italy, 1800–60.
V&A: 90–1868

Earrings such as this, with broad rectangular fronts decorated with rows of pearls, and often filigree, are typical of those worn in Tuscany in the nineteenth century.

110 **Pendent earring**
Gold with applied filigree, length 9.8cm. Venice, Italy, 1812–60.
V&A: 68–1868

The pendant of this earring is hooked loosely onto the wire, as it would have been for Sundays and festivals. Its owner would have worn only the button attached to the wire on working days.

111 **Pendent earring**
Gold, set with foiled pink sapphires and green wax, with strings of pearls, length 8.6cm. Pozzuoli, near Naples, Italy, 1800–60.
V&A: 258–1868

This earring is typical of the luxurious jewellery worn in the area around Naples. The stones have the appearance of rubies and emeralds, but are cheaper substitutes. The loop at the top of the wire is common in traditional earrings. It was tied to a ribbon to help support their weight.

Islamic in origin, but could also date back to Byzantine times.

Having the ear pierced was thought to be beneficial to the individual. It helped to protect children from convulsions and other childhood diseases, and to guard against the ubiquitous evil eye. Consequently, earrings were considered to be amulets in their own right, regardless of their design or decoration. Some men wore earrings, particularly in Sicily, although they usually only wore one at a time, in contrast to women, who always wore them in pairs. There was a widespread belief among seafarers, which was common elsewhere in Europe, that ear piercing and earrings helped improve the eyesight.

Crosses

The strong Catholic tradition in Italy ensured that crosses remained part of the traditional costume. The crosses worn by Italian women include some of the most flamboyant in Europe. Traditional jewellery in general is rarely discreet or understated, but the crosses worn throughout northern and central Italy are impossible to ignore (plate 115). Made of thin gold sheet and up to 40cm in length, they cover the whole front of the body, and when worn, as they frequently were, with matching earrings, would have made an unforgettable display.

Crosses worn as traditional jewellery were always gold in colour, and often attached to one or more matching parts to form an imposing pendant (plate 117). The gold crosses from the area around Turin, which was under French rule from 1640 to 1706, and again during the Napoleonic wars at the beginning of the nineteenth century, have many similarities with French

112 **Hoop earring**
Sheet gold with gold filigree, length 10cm. Naples, Italy, 1832–67.
V&A: 238–1868

Hoop and crescent earrings were common throughout southern Italy. This one comes from Bovino, in Apulia, and has Naples marks. The mix of yellow gold filigree and red sheet gold is also characteristic of the region.

113 **Pendent earring**
Gold with applied filigree and seed pearls, length 5.7cm. Venice, Italy, 1800–50.
V&A: M.78–1909

Earrings such as these are found throughout the old Venetian colonies of the eastern Mediterranean, as well as the area around Venice. Their design may date back to classical times. Venice was famous for its very fine gold filigree work.

crosses. Some are hung from heart-shaped slides, and others from elaborate bow-shaped knots, called a knot of Turin in Savoy in France, while the cross itself is called a cross of Savoy in Italy. In northern Italy, they were set with garnets and pearls as part of a long multi-part pendant, similar to an eighteenth-century stomacher. Women usually wore their crosses hanging from a ribbon, and the topmost part often has a slide loop on the back through which the ribbon passed, rather than a suspension ring.

Crosses were rarely included in necklaces, and where they were the reasons were mainly amuletic or religious. In Sardinia, it is clear from the arrangement of the beads that the necklaces were originally based on rosaries. Sardinian pendent crosses are sometimes made of silver. Elsewhere in Italy, only devotional crosses, which were often crucifixes, were made of silver (plate 116), in contrast to the stylized crosses worn as jewellery, which were invariably of gold. Very few other Italian crosses were crucifixes, that is, crosses carrying a three-dimensional image of the body of Christ.

Amulets and religious pendants

The importance of amulets in Italian traditional jewellery cannot be exaggerated. Amulets can be defined as objects whose sole purpose is to avert possible harm, while talismans attract good fortune, but in practice Italian amulets were expected to perform both kinds of function. In addition to objects worn specifically as amulets, almost

114 **Pendent earring (*Navicella*)**
Gold with applied filigree, length 13.9cm.
Papal States, Italy, 1815–67.
V&A: 48–1868

This earring, called *navicella* because of its ship-like design, was made in the Papal States. It is typical of the town of Sant'Angelo in Vado, where Alessandro Castellani claimed to have found silversmiths still using Etruscan goldsmithing techniques.

115 **Cross pendant**
Sheet gold, length 39.4cm.
Le Marche, Italy, 1820–60.
V&A: 224:1&2–1868

The gold of this pendant has been rolled almost as thin as paper. It comes from the Marche region and would have been worn hanging from a ribbon, with matching earrings.

every aspect of the jewellery worn with traditional dress had an amuletic quality, derived from how and when it was worn, and how it was acquired, as well as its colour, shape, design or material (plate 121).

The most ubiquitous danger, to which Italians seem to have been particularly susceptible, was the evil eye. The *figa* or *manufica* amulet, shaped like a clenched fist with the thumb protruding between the first and second fingers, had been held to be the most effective guard against the evil eye since Roman times. Although this amulet is now considered typically Italian, and is still commonly worn by many men of southern Italian origin today, it was previously used throughout the Mediterranean region. Animals' claws, teeth and tusks protected children from evil spirits, but also acted in a more mundane capacity to help with teething. A uniquely Italian amulet, which was limited to the area around Naples, is the *cimaruta* (plate 118), or sprig of rue. This is a flat openwork pendant made of cast silver in the shape of a stylized branch, with all kinds of protective objects, such as hands, keys and human-faced moons at the ends of the twigs. Its unusual appearance has ensured its continuing popularity to the present day, and copies are still being made, often cast from old examples complete with their original silver marks. Even such basic articles as tooth-and earpicks were transformed into amulets by their shape and decoration.

Religious medallions, often bought at pilgrimage sites and showing images of the appropriate saint (plates 119 and

116 **Cross**
Silver filigree with rock crystal, length 14.3cm. Romagna, Italy, 1800–60.
V&A: 359–1868

This cross would originally have had a relic enclosed in its rock crystal centre. It might have been worn as a pendant, but would more probably have been used for private devotions in the home. It was described as having been 'usually suspended at a bed head' when it was acquired.

117 **Cross pendant**
Gold set with pearls and garnets, length 16cm. Tuscany, Italy, 1800–60.
V&A: 144–1868

Pierced work set with garnets and pearls is characteristic of northern Italy. This cross would have been worn hanging from a ribbon, with matching earrings.

120), or given at baptism by godparents, were widely worn. These were usually set in elaborate filigree mounts.

Because the benefits of protective jewellery of all kinds were additive, they were commonly worn together. It is not unusual to find Christian pendants and non-Christian amulets hung side by side on a rosary, or grouped together on a split ring. Users rarely seem to have discriminated between amulets and religious pendants, which were also worn for their perceived protective and beneficial qualities. Many amulets, descended from pre-Christian times, were adapted to Christian use by attribution to a saint. So the operculum (or closure) of a trochus shell, used against eye diseases since Roman times, was called an eye-stone, or the 'eye of Santa Lucia'. A pendent key amulet, variously attributed to San Valentino or the Holy Spirit, protected against epilepsy.

Necklaces and chains

The universal use of crosses, which were usually worn hanging from chains or ribbons, did not deter Italian women from wearing necklaces as well. The two most common types were strings of beads – of coral (plate 122), glass or metal – and elegant arrangements of decorative chains, plaques and medallions (plate 123), similar to the French *esclavage* (see Chapter 4), which were popular in southern Italy. These were often decorated with filigree or enamel. A very fine supple gold chain (*Manin*), which was highly valued throughout Europe, was made in Venice. In the region around Venice, it formed part of the dowry for everyone rich enough to afford one, and

118 **Amulet (*Cimaruta*)**
Cast silver, length 7.2cm.
South Italy, 1800/1950.
Private collection

The *cimaruta*, or sprig of rue, was a very common amulet in the Naples area. Rue was believed to have strong protective qualities, which were enhanced by the added designs: birds, keys, a human-faced crescent moon, flowers, hands holding hearts. This *cimaruta* has been cast from an old model, and therefore has two sets of silver marks.

119 **Pendant**
Silver medallion in filigree frame, length 7.1cm.
Romagna, Italy, 1800–60.
V&A: 363–1868

The medallion in this pendant represents the Black Madonna of Oropa, a major pilgrimage site in Piedmont. It may have been framed there, or in the Romagna, where it was acquired. The symbol of a double-headed eagle was common throughout Catholic Europe.

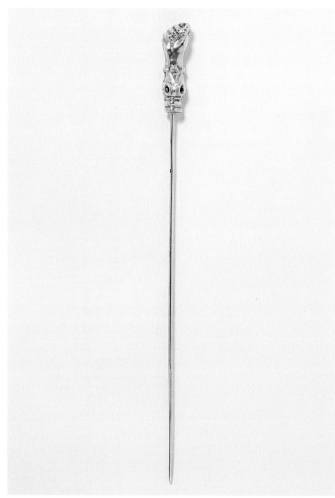

120 **Pendant**
Silver medallion in filigree
frame, length 10.3cm.
Loreto, Le Marche, Italy,
1800–60.
V&A: 339–1890

The medallion in this
pendant shows the *Casa
Santa* (Holy House) of
Loreto, which was a major
pilgrimage site in Le
Marche. Medallions from
pilgrimage sites were often
mounted in filigree.

121 **Hair pin**
Silver, length 27.6cm.
Papal States, Italy, 1815–67.
V&A: 244–1868

The head of this hair pin
is shaped like a very old
amulet called a *manufica*,
resembling a hand making
the fig sign. It was believed
to protect against the evil
eye. The decorative heads of
hair pins often had amuletic
significance.

122 Necklace
Coral beads with silver
terminals and red silk
ribbon, length 32.5cm.
Abruzzo, Italy, 1820–60.
V&A: 225–1868

Coral was popular
throughout Italy. It was
always cut and polished
in the nineteenth century,
rather than left in its natural
state, which was only
used for amulets. The red
silk ribbons are original.
Necklaces were usually
fastened with ribbons, tied
through loops at each end.

123 Necklace
Sheet gold and gold filigree,
with enamel and seed
pearls, length 28.7cm.
Naples, Italy, 1832–5.
V&A: 312–1868

The shape of this necklace
is French in origin, from the
beginning of the nineteenth
century, while the mix of
yellow gold filigree and
red sheet gold is typical
of southern Italian
traditional jewellery.

was usually handed down from mother to daughter. A similar situation existed in Malta, where the gold dowry chain (*gran spinat*) had links decorated with applied filigree. In Sardinia, elaborate cast silver chains, unlike anything worn elsewhere in Italy, were used to fasten a woman's jacket, apron or headdress (plate 124).

Hair pins and head ornaments

The way an Italian woman arranged her hair was as important as the clothes and jewellery she wore in identifying her place in society. Unmarried women were rarely allowed to put their hair up, and were restricted in the kind and number of ornaments they could wear on their head. In many places they were not allowed to wear any.

Throughout the country, married women asserted their status with elaborate hairdos, which almost always involved decorative hair pins. The hairdo was displayed openly in the north, and usually covered in the south. The use of head coverings may have been due to the heat, as British observers thought, but is much more likely to stem from the Spanish, Islamic or even Byzantine heritage of the area. The first time a woman wore the full headdress appropriate to her region was on her wedding day, and there were elaborate rituals associated with this. It was often the bridegroom's privilege to insert or remove the wedding hair pins, and this had great symbolic significance. After the wedding, women wore their hair pins on Sundays, and on other public or festive occasions.

124 **Clasp linked by chains (*Gancera*)**
Cast silver, length 54.5cm. Sardinia, Italy, 1850–1900. Private collection

Gancere are clasps used to fasten the clothing. They were used by men as well as women, on jackets, bodices, aprons and headdresses, often with decorative chains attached. This *gancera* has been altered slightly to change it into a necklace.

125 **Headdress (*Raggiera*)**
Silver, length 12.5–15cm (pins). C. Pirotta (maker), Milan, Italy, *c*.1860. V&A: 388–1868

This *raggiera* headdress comes from the Brianza region of Lombardy. The name means 'like the rays of the sun', because of the way it is arranged round the face. Similar headdresses were worn throughout northern Italy, and in neighbouring Ticino in Switzerland, and the individual pins over an even wider area.

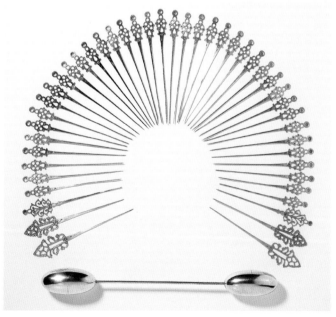

In the north, the hair pins were worn in sets, inserted around the twisted and braided hair, and accompanied by expensive ribbons of silk, embroidery or metallic thread. In Lombardy, it took several hours, and the help of the bride's female relatives and in-laws, to put the full *raggiera* headdress (plates 105 and 125) in place for the wedding; only the pins were taken out at night, so that the bride did not need to go through the whole process again each morning of the marriage period. The time involved in dressing the hair correctly, even if only on special occasions, ensured that elaborate hair ornaments of this kind were among the first articles of traditional jewellery to go out of use. By the end of the nineteenth century, *raggiera* pins were sometimes soldered together to form a single hair comb, but most were discarded completely or converted into tourist souvenirs. Another victim of lack of time was a series of complex gilded filigree hair ornaments worn in the Piedmont region (plate 126). These delicate headbands, barrettes and nets had only been introduced in the mid-nineteenth century, and survived for barely two generations.

In the south, hair pins were much larger, and were worn singly, inserted horizontally through the coiled hair at the back of the head, so that the decorative top of the pin stood out at the side of the face (plates 127 and 128). Many were shaped like miniature swords, called *spatuzze* in the dialect of the south, or had heads which were made like amulets (plates 121 and 129), to give added protection to the wearer.

126 **Headdress (*Burletto*)**
Silver-gilt filigree, width
12cm. Novara, Piedmont,
Italy, 1870–1900.
V&A: M.527–1924
(Given by Estella and
Enrico Canziani)

This *burletto* was worn on
the back of the head, held
in place by hair pins with
long filigree pendants,
and accompanied by a
matching band across the
forehead. The net backing
is typical of the filigree of
Piedmont. Estella Canziani
was a strong proponent of
traditional costume, and
painted the portrait in
plate 91.

127 **Hair pin**
(*Limoncello e carofano*)
Silver filigree, length
25.5cm. Naples, Italy,
1835–63.
V&A: 289–1868

Hair pins with round filigree
tops were found throughout
Italy. This design, called
limoncello e carofano (a little
lemon with a sprouting top),
is typical of southern Italy.
Similar hair pins are also
found across the Adriatic
in Dalmatia.

Buttons

The buttons, worn by men and women at collar and cuff as well as to fasten their shirts and jackets, are one of the elements which make Sardinian traditional jewellery so distinctive. Silver buttons were part of men's costume in many other areas of southern Italy formerly under Spanish rule, but were no longer used by the mid-nineteenth century. In Malta, silver buttons were the most distinctive item of traditional jewellery to survive: round, in imitation filigree, in the eighteenth century, and conical in the nineteenth (plate 130). Similar conical buttons were worn by men in the area around Naples and possibly in Sicily, and this distinctive pattern drifted across the narrow sea to Libya, where it first appeared in the nineteenth century as buttons on women's Ottoman dress, before becoming a head ornament by the twentieth century. Neapolitan men also wore open-backed buttons shaped like bee hives or shallow cones.

By the end of the nineteenth century, all trace of these buttons had vanished on the mainland, except for a few which can still be seen decorating the clothing of the shepherds in *presepi* (Christmas crib) scenes, who traditionally wore the costume of the local peasants.

In Abruzzo, silver buttons were worn by both men and women until well into the twentieth century at places such as Scanno.

128 **Gala dress of Frosolone, Molise, Italy**
From *Il costume populare in Italia*, E. Calderini (Milan, 1934)

This woman is wearing a large silver filigree hair pin in her hair, and a selection of gold necklaces. The lowest necklace, of beads, is pinned to two silk rosettes at the side of her bodice, rather than hanging from her neck.

129 **Hair pin**
Silver, length 20.5cm. Naples, Italy, 1832–67. V&A: 230–1868

This hair pin is typical of the region around Naples. The hand holding a flower at the top was intended to protect the wearer, and is related to the *manufica* amulet (plate 121). The two slits were threaded with ribbons to hold it firmly in place.

130 **Toggle button**
Silver with applied filigree, diam. 1.7cm. Malta, 1801–9. V&A: 1467E–1873

Toggle buttons, with a short T-shaped bar permanently attached to the button, were used throughout the Mediterranean region. This conical button is typical of those from Malta. It would have been worn by a man, six or 12 at a time, to fasten his waistcoat.

Spain and Portugal

The design of most traditional jewellery in the Iberian Peninsula is firmly Catholic, and most patterns go back no further than the sixteenth century. This jewellery is mainly made of gold, silver-gilt, or gilt metal. But there is also an older strand, often found in jewellery from places in the interior, such as Extremadura and Léon, which is more usually expressed in silver, rather than gold, and includes traces of Celtic, Visigothic and Moorish influence (plate 131).

Iberian traditional jewellery, in its turn, influenced traditional jewellery elsewhere in the world. This was due both to the dominance of Spanish fashion in the sixteenth and early seventeenth centuries, and to the unique status of Spain and Portugal as colonial powers. Although other nations, including the Dutch, British, French and Danish, had settlements outside Europe in the seventeenth century, the extent and duration of the Spanish empire, as well as the distinctiveness of the jewellery which was worn by the *peninsulares* (those born in Europe), made a lasting impression in many parts of Central and South America and southeast Asia.

This process of foreign influence may have started even earlier, before the European colonization of America, with the expulsion from Spain of the Jews and Moors in 1492. Many of them, including skilled goldsmiths, settled among their co-religionists in existing communities in North Africa. They are often credited with introducing the practice of enamelling, which survives to this day in parts of the Maghreb. There is a much clearer link to the design of many pieces of traditional jewellery, particularly in Morocco, which clearly

131 **Gala costume from La Alberca, Salamanca**
From *Regional costumes of Spain*, Isobel De Palencia (London, 1926)

The heavy silver necklaces of this costume are characteristic of the village of La Alberca. They were tied to the dress at the back, to relieve the weight on the wearer's neck. She is also wearing large silver toggle buttons on her raised sleeve.

share common roots with Iberian jewellery.

One of the main characteristics of Iberian traditional jewellery is the use of filigree (plate 133). Filigree in the modern style, possibly originating in China, arrived at Lisbon from the Portuguese outposts in Macao and Goa, and at Seville from the Philippines via Mexico, in the early sixteenth century. From there, it rapidly spread across the rest of Europe. At first filigree was restricted to luxury items, but it was quickly adopted for religious objects, and had spread to all kinds of traditional jewellery by the eighteenth century. The main Iberian centres were at Cordoba and Salamanca in Spain, and in northern Portugal, where filigree survives as a living tradition to this day.

Earrings

Earrings were the most numerous and widespread type of traditional jewellery in the Peninsula, and all Spanish and Portuguese women wore them. Their use in Spain may be Moorish in origin, as they continued to be worn there during the Middle Ages, unlike in many other Catholic countries. Certainly the name most commonly used for a pendent earring, *arracada*, is Arabic in origin.

Perhaps as a result, the difference between the various strands of influence in Iberian traditional jewellery is at its most obvious in the earrings. In the coastal provinces along the Atlantic and Mediterranean shores, and in the cities, they were usually baroque in form, descended from the aristocratic jewellery of the seventeenth and eighteenth centuries. These earrings were large pendent *girandole* (plate 132) or drop

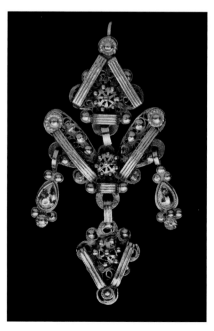

132 **Earring**
Gilt metal set with mirror glass pastes, length 7cm. Saragossa, Spain, 1800–70.
V&A: 417–1873

The *girandole* design of this earring is found in many parts of Europe from the seventeenth to the nineteenth centuries, but the use of mirror glass is characteristic of Spanish traditional jewellery. It would have been worn with a matching pendant.

133 **Earring**
Silver-gilt filigree, length 8cm. Santiago de Compostela, Galicia, Spain, *c.*1870.
V&A: 1166–1873

The design of this earring is based on the seventeenth-century *girandole* earring, with three drops hanging from a central plaque. The filigree and strapwork technique make it unique to Santiago. It would have been worn with a matching pendant.

shapes, often studded with gems, or glass pastes imitating gems (plate 135). Although red and white were widely used, jewellery with green stones was worn everywhere, particularly in Valencia (see plate 142). The popularity of green stones in Iberia may date from the discovery of emeralds in Colombia in the sixteenth century, but it may also reflect earlier Muslim preferences for the colour, before the Reconquista of 1492. The main exception is in Catalonia, whose jewellery has as much in common with that of the south of France as with the rest of Spain. Here red is more common, particularly in the long articulated earrings which are the most characteristic piece of jewellery in the region (plate 134). Similar earrings were worn elsewhere in the Peninsula, although rarely of the same length. In Portugal and neighbouring Galicia, the lowest part of the drop design became wider and rounder, creating a distinctive earring which is still widely worn today (plates 137 and 139).

In contrast, the earrings of the interior, from places such as Zamora, are totally different (plate 136), with shapes which are often unique in Europe, although sometimes familiar to this day in the traditional jewellery of other continents. The crescent-shaped earrings of Astorga, with green pastes on the side and bird pendants (plate 138), are closely linked to those worn in Morocco. Similarly, the cast triangular pendants worn on earrings in Salamanca and Zamora (plate 140) call to mind the hand-shaped amulets of the Maghreb; the Spanish name for these earrings, *de mano*, meaning hand, only emphasizes the resemblance. Many of the early Hispanic emigrants to Central and South America came from these regions, and their earrings

134 **Earring**
Gold set with foiled hessonite garnets, length 14cm. Barcelona, Spain, 1865–70.
V&A: 1084A–1871

This earring is basically a *girandole* in design, but it has been lengthened and narrowed to a shape which is typical of Catalonia. Earrings such as this were often set with red stones, which were usually backed with foil to improve their colour.

135 **Earring**
Silver with mirror glass pastes, length 10.4cm. Barcelona, Spain, 1865–70.
V&A: 1239A–1871

The long, narrow articulated shape of this earring is typical of those worn in Catalonia. It would originally have had a third drop hanging from the tip. The silver surrounds of the mirror glass pastes have been facetted to imitate cut-steel or gems.

136 Earring
(*Pendiente de calabaza*)
Silver-gilt filigree with red
silk, length 12.2cm. Astorga,
León, Spain, 1800–70.
V&A: 1116A–1873

This earring is named a
'gourd' for its shape, and
was traditionally lined with
a piece of red cloth. It is
typical of the province of
León. The S-shaped link
and the little pendent doves
are found on many types of
earring from that region.

137 Earring (*Pendiente de reloj*)
Silver-gilt filigree, length
7.5cm. Galicia, Spain,
*c.*1870.
V&A: 414–1873

This earring, called a
'clock' in Spanish due to its
appearance, comes from
Galicia. Identical earrings
are found across the border
in northern Portugal, where
they are called *a rainha*, or
'of the queen'. They are one
of the most characteristic
types of Portuguese
traditional earring, and are
still being made today.

138 Earring
Silver-gilt set with a green
paste, length 4.8cm,
Astorga, León, Spain,
1800–70.
V&A: 1113–1873

This earring is typical of
those worn in the province
of León. Its design may date
back to Moorish times, and
similar designs are common
in Morocco to this day. The
little pendent dove is often
found on jewellery from
León and Salamanca.

139 Woman in traditional Portuguese dress
From *Peoples of all Nations*
(London, *c.*1930)

This woman is wearing
the traditional jewellery
of northern Portugal:
necklaces of gold beads,
a religious pendant, and
the characteristic *a rainha*
pierced earrings. She
would only have dressed
as sumptuously as this on
Sundays and for festivals.

have in turn influenced the jewellery of Latin America. The little pendant points, a common feature of Spanish jewellery from the interior, are one of the main characteristics of the *charros* jewellery of Mexico, and the cast silver earrings of Salamanca (plate 141) are mirrored, and enhanced, in the earrings and other pendants of the Mapuche of Chile. Crescent earrings can be seen widely to this day in the urban jewellery of Mexico and the Philippines.

As in other countries where earrings were worn, they have a strong symbolic value. In the north of Portugal, a woman appearing without earrings was assumed to have made a serious vow of abstention. In Spain, different kinds of earrings showed whether a woman was married or unmarried, or even denoted a wet-nurse.

Crosses

The cross is the most imposing piece of jewellery in the Iberian region. Spanish traditional crosses have a number of different patterns. Many are large and elaborate, in eighteenth-century style (plate 142), and are often decorated with filigree (plate 143) and set with gems or their imitations. These crosses were highly stylized (plate 144), and made to match the other jewellery of their owners, particularly the earrings. They were usually worn on a ribbon round the neck, which was threaded through the bars on the back of the top part. Smaller, more functional, crosses were usually attached to rosaries. These were often crucifixes, with a cast image of the body of Christ on the cross, and were made of cast gold or gilded metal, or

140 **Earring**
Silver-gilt, length 9.5cm.
Salamanca, Spain, 1800–70.
V&A: 1154–1873

Earrings with heavy cast pierced triangular pendants are typical of inland Spain. The pendants originally hung from large plain wire hoops, but this has a smaller heavy cast hoop. The shape of the pendant is reminiscent of the *hamsa* amulets of North Africa.

141 **Earring**
Silver, length 5.5cm.
Salamanca, Spain, 1800–70.
V&A: 1121–1873

Cast silver earrings, often with small pendants, were worn throughout inland Spain. This particular design may be the origin of the silver earrings worn by the Mapuche of Chile.

142 **Cross pendant**
Silver, partly gilded, with green pastes, length 15.5cm. Valencia, Spain, 1800–70.
V&A: 111–1870

Crosses of eighteenth-century design were worn throughout Spain. The use of green stones was also very common, particularly in Valencia. This cross is set with green pastes, imitating the emeralds used in aristocratic jewellery.

143 **Cross pendant**
Silver-gilt filigree, length 14.8cm. Salamanca, Spain, 1800–70.
V&A: 1124–1873

Salamanca was famous for its filigree work in the nineteenth century, and still produces it today. This cross pendant of delicate silver-gilt filigree imitates an eighteenth-century gem-set original.

filigree to match the rosary beads. An older kind of crucifix, made of heavy cast silver, and probably dating back to a medieval prototype, survived in Castile and León (plate 145).

Rosaries, religious pendants and amulets

The use of spiritual aids as jewellery was universal. Relics and images from pilgrimage centres such as Santiago de Compostela, or the Virgin of the Pillar at Saragossa, were mounted in frames of twisted wire or filigree. One of the earliest uses of filigree was for rosary beads and crucifixes. Spanish rosaries often have a flat filigree rosette as a paternoster, instead of the large bead used in other countries, and the crucifixes are often made of filigree in a cylindrical shape (plate 146). In the northwest of Spain, and across the border in northern Portugal, the most distinctive pendant is a large gold heart, representative of divine as well as romantic love, with a curved point and a stylized crown above. It always takes the same shape, regardless of whether it is flat or hollow (plate 147), of sheet gold or filigree (plate 148).

In the central regions of Spain, where the jewellery was traditionally made of heavy silver, women wore religious pendants and medallions which could be up to 15cm in diameter (plate 150). These were worn singly on ribbons or, more often, as the centrepiece of a necklace of coral or silver beads with other pendants. At the little village of La Alberca, near Salamanca (see plate 131), the customary wedding necklace was so long and heavy as to be almost unwearable (plate 149). Its individual parts provide evidence of its ancestry:

144 **Cross pendant**
Gold filigree with baroque and seed pearls, length 14.7cm. Salamanca, Spain, 1800–70.
V&A: 1375–1873

This silver-gilt filigree cross is eighteenth century in design, but the lavish use of irregular pearls is typical of the traditional jewellery made in Salamanca. Its matching earrings can be seen at the V&A.

145 **Crucifix (*Cruceta*)**
Silver, length 7.4cm. Astorga, León, Spain, 1650–1750.
V&A: 1120–1873

This heavy cast silver crucifix comes from Astorga, but the design was used throughout inland Spain. It would have been worn on a bead necklace, often with other religious pendants. The wide barrel-shaped loop is found on many pendants from inland Spain made before the nineteenth century.

146 Crucifix (*Cristo de Burgos*)
Silver filigree, partly gilded,
length 10.2cm. Burgos,
Castile, Spain, 1750–1800.
V&A: 114–1870

This crucifix was probably
worn on a rosary. The long
pleated skirt of Christ is
characteristic of Hispanic
crucifixes, and can also
be found widely in Latin
America. The tubular
filigree construction of the
cross is typical of Spanish
crucifixes.

147 Heart pendant
Sheet gold with applied
filigree, length 7.6cm.
Oporto, north Portugal,
1800–70.
V&A: 1074–1873

Pendent crowned hearts,
always with a slight curve
to the tip, are characteristic
of northern Portugal. They
were also made across
the border in neighbouring
Spanish Galicia. They are
always made of gold,
or gilded metal, and
represent religious as
well as secular values.

148 Heart pendant
Gold filigree, length 10.6cm.
Oporto, north Portugal,
c.1860.
V&A: 1073–1873

The crowned heart
pendants typical of northern
Portugal are always the
same shape, whether they
are made of sheet gold or
filigree. Filigree is still one
of the specialities of the
Oporto region.

the round and heart-shaped pendants are late medieval in pattern, while the design of the tubular beads with crenellated ends may be even earlier, dating back to the period of Moorish rule. Similar beads were still being worn in Morocco by the descendants of the Andalusian Moors as late as the nineteenth century.

In addition to pendants which were specifically Christian, amulets were in common use. Many pre-dated the Christian era in design and function, such as the crescent moon, often with a human face, or the *higa*, a clenched fist with the thumb sticking out between the first two fingers (plate 151). This was a popular amulet throughout the Mediterranean region as a protection against the evil eye. By the nineteenth century the use of amulets was largely restricted to the urban poor and conservative rural people, but it had previously been common among all classes, as can be seen in seventeenth-century portraits of royal children wearing richly mounted chestnuts, badger's paws and branches of coral. Amulets such as these were still in widespread use in nineteenth-century Spain.

Combs, hair pins and head ornaments

As elsewhere in Europe, the way a woman dressed her hair was the most important way in which she announced to the world her status and identity. Married women usually wore their hair up, coiled into buns at either side of the face, and often secured by decorative combs and hair pins. They always wore some kind of head covering or wrap, which ranged from a light piece of embroidered silk or lace to a heavy wool shawl. In some

149 **Necklace (*Vuelta grande*)**
Silver, silver-gilt, and silver-plated copper, with filigree and applied filigree, length 130cm. La Alberca, Salamanca, Spain, 1600–1900.
V&A: M.53:1&2–1856
(Given by Dr W.L. Hildburgh)

This long heavy necklace was worn by brides in the village of La Alberca, near Salamanca. It is very old in concept: some of the religious medallions were probably made in the seventeenth century, and the design of the tubular beads dates back to the time of the Moors.

150 **Pendant (*Cristo barrigon or preñao*)**
Cast silver-gilt with applied filigree, diam. 13.2cm. Astorga, León, Spain, 1700–99.
V&A: 1377–1873

Heavy silver religious pendants are typical of inland Spain. This pendant looks as if it might originally have been a reliquary, but there is no evidence that it ever opened. The name, meaning pot-bellied, or pregnant, refers to its shape as much as to its use as an amulet during pregnancy.

151 **Amulet (*Higa*)**
Carved jet set in silver, length 12.4cm. Spain, 1800–1900.
V&A: M.22–1917
(Given by Dr W.L. Hildburgh)

The *higa* amulet, also common in southern Italy, was believed to avert the evil eye. Its power was increased by the carved image of a moon with a human face, and the use of jet. Jet is native to northwest Spain, and was widely used for centuries for both amulets and religious objects.

places this eliminated the possibility of any kind of head jewellery, but in others, particularly in the south of Spain, the scarf was worn over the pins and combs. The use of a high comb, worn at the back of the head, was common throughout Spain, and may have been influenced by Chinese fashions, transmitted from goldsmiths working in Spanish Mexico or the Philippines. Because the comb was the most important part of the headdress, Spanish hair pins are usually smaller than those used in other parts of Catholic Europe, and worn in sets, to accompany the comb, rather than singly.

The hair ornaments of Valencia were particularly complex (plate 153). The woman wound half her hair into a chignon at the back of the head, secured by a pair of long interlocking pins (plate 152) and supporting a high back comb on top

(plate 154). She used the rest of her hair to create two smaller buns, at either side of the head over the ears. These each had six smaller matching pins inserted around the perimeter, with a smaller comb, matching that at the back, stuck into the top. She finished off the hairdo with a large pair of pendent earrings. Over time, the early flat top of the comb became larger, rounded and more elaborate, and this is the form which is worn today in Valencia for the annual *fallas* parades in honour of St Joseph and the end of winter. The high back comb of Andalusia, usually made of tortoiseshell rather than metal, was thought typical of Spanish jewellery in Britain in the nineteenth century, and was very fashionable as eveningwear there in the early 1870s.

152 **Pair of hair pins**
Silver-gilt set with green pastes, length 21.5cm. Valencia, Spain, 1865–70. V&A: 691–1870

These hair pins were used to support the chignon at the back of the head. They slotted into each other to prevent them falling out. The Valencians were fond of green stones, and used them in much of their jewellery.

153 **How the hair is dressed in Valencia**
From *Regional costumes of Spain*, Isobel De Palencia (London, 1926)

The hairdo of Valencia was one of the most elaborate in Spain. It was held in place by a set of three silver combs, and numerous hair pins, often set with green pastes. The pendent earrings completed the effect.

154 Comb

Silver-plated copper, partly gilded, width 16.5cm. Valencia, Spain, 1865–70. V&A: 683–1870

This comb was worn stuck into the top of a chignon, with a smaller matching comb at each side. It is made of copper, which has been silver-plated and then gilded, to make it look like silver-gilt.

Buttons

As elsewhere in Europe, Spanish men wore large numbers of decorative buttons on their sleeves and collars, on the outer seams of their trousers, and profusely down the front of their shirts, jackets and coats. Most were of filigree, but in Salamanca men also wore round and octagonal flat buttons (plate 155), and domed hollow buttons decorated with granulation and filigree. Spanish women also wore buttons of delicate silver filigree, often gilded (plate 157), or heavy toggle buttons (plate 156) along the seams of their sleeves (see plate 131). In addition, both men and women employed tiny filigree buttons, sometimes hundreds at a time, to accentuate the design of their outer clothing, inserting their toggle bars through the cloth like pins along the curves of the pattern. Most Spanish buttons were not sewn directly on the clothing, but attached by a toggle, a short bar joined permanently to the button by a flexible link. This kind of fitting spread from Spain through much of Mediterranean Europe, including southern Italy and the neighbouring islands as far as the eastern coasts of the Adriatic.

155 Toggle button

Silver, diam. 2.9cm. Cordoba, Spain, 1865–70. V&A: 1177–1871

Large flat toggle buttons were worn by men in double rows on their waistcoats. This one was made in Cordoba, and has the lion silver mark of Cordoba on its back. Buttons such as these are typical of the costume of Salamanca.

156 Toggle button

Silver filigree, length 8.2cm. Murcia, Spain, 1865–70. V&A: 731C–1870

Silver filigree toggle buttons were worn throughout Spain by men, women and children, in a wide range of sizes and designs. Large, heavy buttons such as these were usually worn by women, six at a time, on their sleeves.

157 Pair of linked buttons

Silver-gilt filigree, diam. 2.5cm. Salamanca, Spain, c.1850. V&A: 1126–1873

These filigree buttons with sheet metal backs were probably worn as cuff or collar links. Both men and women wore filigree buttons, but those worn by women are usually larger.

The Eastern Frontier

From Russia to the Balkans and Greece

This region stretches from European Russia in the north to the Balkan Peninsula and the Greek islands in the south. It has the most complex political and cultural history of any region in Europe, and traces of the ebb and flow of many very different cultures survive in its traditional jewellery, ranging from the pagan migratory Slavs to the hieratic Byzantine inheritors of classical Greek and Roman culture. The common factor which binds the region together is its long history of struggle against, and occupation by, its eastern, non-Christian neighbours, at first the Mongols, and later the Ottoman Turks. This resulted in a strong eastern influence on clothing and jewellery, which was immediately apparent to western visitors, if not always to the wearers themselves, who tended to concentrate on specific local differences.

In eastern Europe and Russia, men's costume tended to be looser and longer than elsewhere in Europe, and necessitated large numbers of buttons, which could be very large and decorative. Although banned at the Russian court by Tsar Peter the Great in 1700, traditional male dress continued in use by the aristocracy in other countries, in various forms, until the nineteenth century. Male costume in the Balkans, where Ottoman rule continued longest, was a mix of indigenous dress and Turkish urban influence.

The women's traditional costume was also much looser than that worn in western Europe, often including layers of long, straight garments, with or without sleeves. The ubiquitous laced bodice of western Europe was only worn in places where western influences were strong. In the Balkans,

158 **Russian peasant woman,** *c.*1820
From *Russian Jewellery, 16th–20th Centuries*, Historical Museum Moscow (Moscow, 1987)

The most distinctive elements of Russian traditional jewellery are the earrings, and the headdresses made of freshwater pearls. The earrings may be Slav in origin – they are quite unlike any others in Europe. This woman is also wearing a long filigree chain, another piece which is typically Russian.

7

women were more likely to wear a short stiff jacket or waistcoat, smothered in gold embroidery and fastened by hooks or clasps.

The specific demands of this eastern clothing resulted in a range of forms and uses which are quite different from the jewellery worn elsewhere in Europe. As with the clothing, a major influence on the jewellery of the region was eastern – Mongol in Russia, Ottoman to the south. It is sometimes difficult to disentangle Ottoman from Byzantine influence, as one of the main influences on Islamic jewellery itself was the jewellery of the Byzantine Empire.

More jewellery was worn in the Balkans than elsewhere in the region, although the quality of the materials was often poor. The most important elements were clasps, head ornaments and chains. In Russia, traditional chains, earrings and buttons continued in use up to the beginning of the twentieth century, augmented with fashionable brooches, bracelets and necklaces.

There is usually very little difference between the jewellery of any one faith in the region, and that of their neighbours of other religions, including Muslims and Jews, as well as Catholic, Protestant and Orthodox Christians. Only the details of design display their owners' beliefs.

Headdresses

The headdress was the most important element of a woman's costume, because it declared her status. In eastern Europe, an unmarried girl wore her hair loose, or uncovered, as in many other places in Europe. The first time she put on a head covering was on her wedding day. It asserted her purity, and was decorated with special ornaments to mark the occasion, and the new phase in her life. Head ornaments of various kinds, such as the *prochelnik* diadem (plate 159) worn in Bulgaria, were usually a compulsory element of the dowry. Brides of all faiths wore head ornaments at their wedding, but diadems and crowns, descended from Byzantine court jewellery, were only worn by Christian women. After the ceremonies ended, the new bride dressed her hair like a married woman, and continued to wear the jewellery appropriate to that state for the rest of her life.

In the Balkans, married women wore scarves on their heads, ranging from light silk veils to heavy woollen cloths capable of protecting them from the worst of the winter weather. They usually fastened these scarves with hooks, often linked by chains and decorated with pendent coins and amulets. Hair pins were less common, limited to the area of Italian influence along the Adriatic coast, parts of Bulgaria, and some of the islands, including Cyprus. In some places, women wore a small cap, like a fez, with a round silver disc sewn to its top. This was Ottoman in origin, as its name *tepelik* ('little hill' in Turkish) indicates, although it was worn equally by all religious groups. In Russia, women wore a headdress covered with seed pearl embroidery (plate 158), which was so emblematic that it was ordained as part of the official court dress for women by Catherine the Great in 1782. A woman's head wearing one variant, a *kokoshnik*, was used as the standard mark for Russian silver from the end of the nineteenth century until the 1920s.

159 **Diadem (*Prochelnik*)**
Silver-gilt set with blue pastes, length 34.6cm.
Preslav, eastern Bulgaria, *c*.1850.
V&A: 1285–1873

The *prochelnik* was a diadem, first worn by the bride at her wedding, and only used by married women. It was fastened across the forehead by a ribbon tied to the loops at each end. It originated in Byzantine aristocratic jewellery, and was found in Greece as well as Bulgaria.

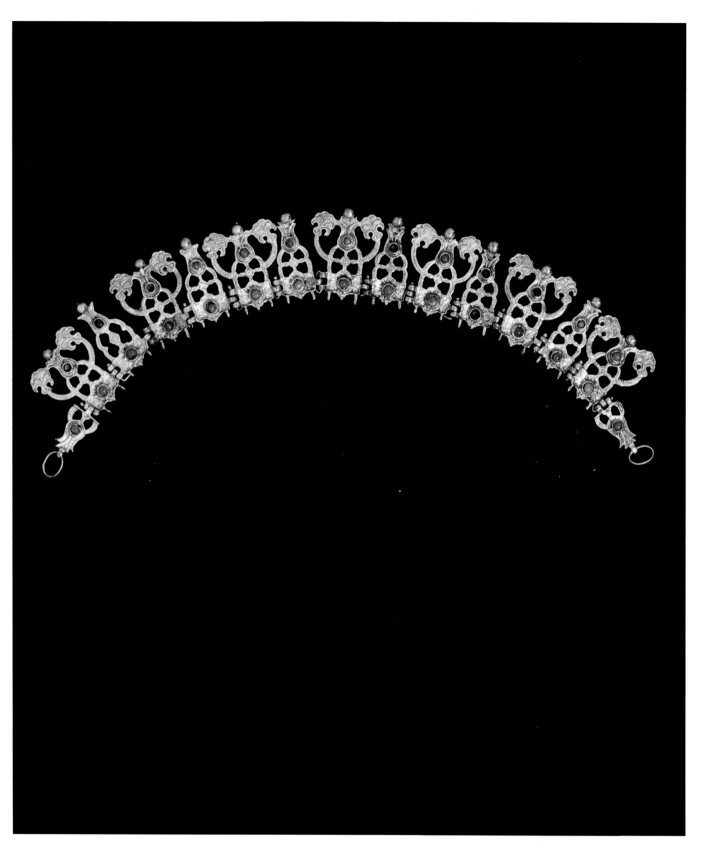

Earrings and ear ornaments

Earrings were worn by all women in eastern Europe. Their design mainly dates back to Byzantine times, with the exception of some worn along the coast of Dalmatia and in the Greek islands, which are more Italian in form (see plate 112), and the distinctive Russian earrings of pendent beads (plate 158), which are probably Slav in origin (plates 160, 161 and 162). Most are long and articulated, often hinged together rather than linked by small rings, and strictly geometric in shape (plate 163). They were intended to frame the face (plate 164), together with a diadem or band across the forehead, in a way that is familiar from many Byzantine mosaics and wall paintings, as well as traditional Islamic dress. Those that were too large to hang comfortably from the ear had hooks instead of wires, which were fastened above the ear in the headdress, the scarf or the hair (plate 167). Earrings, in Russia or further south, were often linked together by decorative chains which hung down under the chin, or over or round the back of the head, secured by small hooks (plate 165). These sharp, decorative hooks are very characteristic of Balkan jewellery.

Another common Balkan design, which is found mainly in Bulgaria, but also in Bosnia and Serbia, is a round stud earring, shaped like the rays of the sun, which was sometimes set with gems or pearls (plate 166). This design may date back to the prehistoric inhabitants of the region.

The interchangeable nature of earrings and ear ornaments suggests that the act of piercing the ear was less important than the finished appearance and placing of the jewellery

160 **Pair of earrings (*Golubtsi*)**
Silver-gilt with red and blue pastes and silver-plated beads, length 6.1cm. Russia, 1800–80. V&A: 527&A–1883

These earrings are called *golubtsi* (dove) because they resemble a stylized bird. The design has remained largely unchanged since the seventeenth century.

161 **Pair of earrings**
Silver with seed pearls and orange glass bead, length 4.2cm. Russia, 1800–80. V&A: 530&A–1883

Earrings with beads strung on vertical wires are among the most common types of Russian traditional earring. The beads are often arranged asymmetrically. The seed pearls came from freshwater molluscs found in local rivers.

162 **Pair of earrings (*Troichatki*)**
Silver-plated copper with glass beads, length 7.9cm. Russia, 1800–80. V&A: 538&A–1883

Troichatki means three, and refers to the number of pendants. These earrings are made of silver-plated copper, but silver earrings would have looked exactly the same. Earrings of this type are almost never marked, whatever material they are made of.

163 Earring
Silver-gilt with applied
filigree, pastes and coral,
length 10cm.
Balkans, *c*.1850.
V&A: 580–1868

This earring, one of a pair,
was bought at the French
International Exhibition
of 1867 as an example of
modern Turkish work. It
was probably made in the
Balkans, under Turkish
rule at the time, as were
other pieces bought with it.

**164 Macedonian girl
from Struga**
From *Peoples of all Nations*
(London, *c*.1930)

This girl from Struga may
be dressed in her wedding
finery. She is wearing a pair
of long pendent earrings
linked by a chain under the
chin, another chain across
her forehead to hold her
scarf in place, and further
chains and clasps on
her bodice.

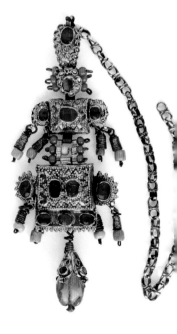

165 Pair of linked earrings
Silver with red glass beads,
length 92.2cm. Albania,
c.1850.
V&A: 1429&A–1873

Earrings in the Balkans
were frequently linked
together by chains. The
chain could hang under the
chin, round the back of the
head, or over the forehead.
The hook in the centre
would have been fastened
into the clothing.

166 Earring (*Arpalii*)
Silver-gilt with coral, length
4.1cm. Bulgaria, *c.*1850.
V&A: 1291–1873

This *arpalii* earring comes
from Bulgaria, although
similar shapes are found
throughout the Balkan
region. The thick circular
wire, often with a short
length of decoration
at the front, is typical of
Slav earrings.

167 Pair of ear ornaments
Silver-gilt with applied
filigree and red, green and
turquoise pastes, length
10.8cm. Bosnia, 1800–50.
Private collection

These ornaments are
derived from earrings, as
can be seen from the pastes
on the side of the hoop.
Over time they grew larger
and heavier, and were
hung directly from the
headdress. By the end
of the nineteenth century
they were suspended
on long ribbons over the
breast, sometimes
reaching to the waist.

around the head. Even so, there were many traditions
associated with pierced ears. Perhaps the most important
was the practice found in many places of putting earrings in
the ears of baby boys, particularly when the mother had
had previous difficulties in pregnancy and childbirth, or her
children had died young. It was hoped that any evil spirits
would overlook the child as a worthless girl. In Muslim
(and Jewish) belief, pierced ears were a sign of slavery, and
therefore normally inappropriate for boys or men.

Belts and clasps

A belt was an integral part of the bride's dress in many
European countries. Its use in the wedding ceremony dates
back to the late Middle Ages, and the bridegroom often
unfastens it as the final gesture before retiring with the
bride. The use of these belts, richly made of interlocking
silver plaques, or appliqués or slides mounted on leather or
velvet, only survived in a few places in the Balkans, including
Dalmatia and Thrace, in the nineteenth century. Everywhere
else they were superseded during the years of Ottoman rule
by clasps.

The waist clasp, usually worn on an embroidered cloth
belt, was the most ubiquitous piece of women's jewellery in
the Balkans. It was a compulsory part of the dowry and the
marriage ceremony, and every married woman would have
worn one, of brass or plated metal if she could not afford silver.
Unlike some other types of jewellery, they were not reserved
for festive occasions, but were worn on a daily basis. They

are almost certainly Ottoman in origin (plate 168). There is no evidence of their use during the Byzantine Empire, in Russia, or in the numerous colonies of Albanians in Italy, who fled before the Ottoman invasion, and the main shapes, of tulips and the comma pattern familiar from Indian textiles but dating back to Sassanian times in Persia, must have come from the east. A few are small and nondescript, but the majority are large, flamboyant and extravagantly decorated, with applied filigree and coloured pastes, and pendent chains, coins and dangles (plate 169).

These clasps were made in a number of clearly defined patterns, but it is difficult to locate them precisely. Outside the lands of the Austro-Hungarian Empire, in the north of the Balkans, there was no established system of marking silver, and much of that used for clasps was of a very low standard anyway, often containing less than 50 per cent silver mixed with copper and other cheaper metals. The silversmiths often added arsenic to the alloy, to counteract the yellow of the copper.

As the silversmiths who made the bulk of the traditional jewellery were usually partly itinerant, travelling throughout the Balkans from spring to autumn taking orders and selling ready-made stock, clasps of similar appearance were worn in many different places. Even so, some generalizations can be made. Filigree clasps, shaped like a trio of tulips, are most common in the northwest of the Balkans, and on the Greek islands, including Cyprus (plate 170). Filigree was a comparatively late technique, rarely used before the late eighteenth century, and

168 **Clasp**
Silver and niello, width 16.2cm. Cyprus, 1650–1750. V&A: 1537-1888

The clasp was the most important piece of jewellery for Balkan women. This clasp is made of silver decorated with niello, a black metallic compound inlaid in silver which was popular in Russia and the Balkans. The decoration of roses and tulips is typically Ottoman in character.

169 **Clasp**
Silver-gilt plated metal with applied filigree and red pastes, width 22cm. Macedonia or Thessaly, Greece, 1850–1900. Private collection

---

Clasps of this design originally came from northern Greece, but were later worn in Attica. This example is made of metal which has been double plated with gold over silver, a common technique for Balkan jewellery in the nineteenth century. It was worn by a woman to fasten her belt (see plate 1).

170 **Clasp**
Silver-gilt filigree with red and green pastes, width 20.5cm. Cyprus, 1750–1850. V&A: 1528:1&2-1888

This clasp is shaped like three stylized tulips or pomegranates, a favourite Balkan motif which is probably Ottoman in origin. It is typical of the fine filigree work of Cyprus.

171 Clasp
Silver-gilt filigree with coral,
width 16.3cm. Balkans,
1800–50.
V&A: 952–1884

The two sides of this clasp
are shaped like stylized
tulips or pomegranates.
The inlaid pieces of striated
coral, known as 'finger
nails', are typical of the
work of Saphrampolis in
northern Anatolia. They
were esteemed throughout
the Balkans.

172 Clasp
Silver-gilt filigree with
enamel and a blue paste,
width 23.5cm. Cyprus,
1750–1850.
V&A: 1530&A–1888

The shape of this clasp is
one of the most popular in
the Balkan region, and is
derived from the Persian
'*boteh*' pattern. The delicate
filigree enamel, usually in
shades of blue and green, is
typical of Cypriot work.

173 Clasp
Silver and mother-of-pearl
with coloured inlay,
width 19cm. Balkans,
1850–1900.
Private collection

Plaques of carved mother-
of-pearl were imported from
the Holy Land, where there
was a thriving industry in
religious souvenirs. They
were worn as women's
belt clasps throughout the
Balkan region. This clasp
may have belonged to an
Orthodox priest, because of
its religious theme.

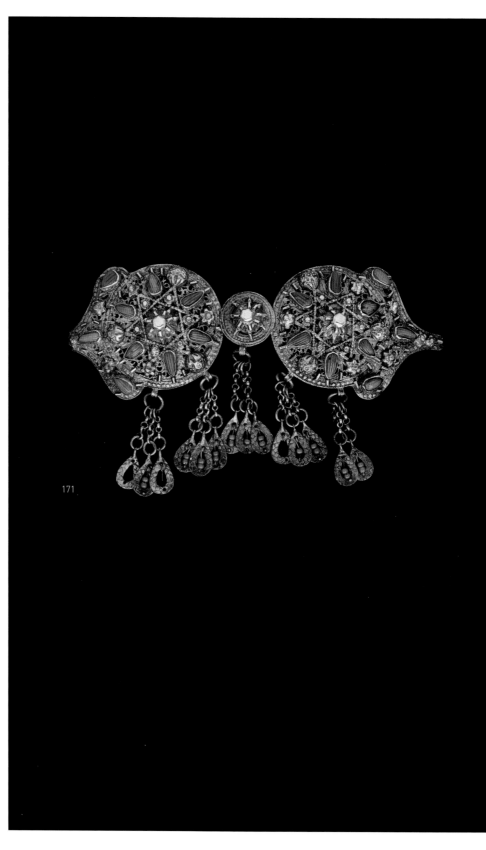

171

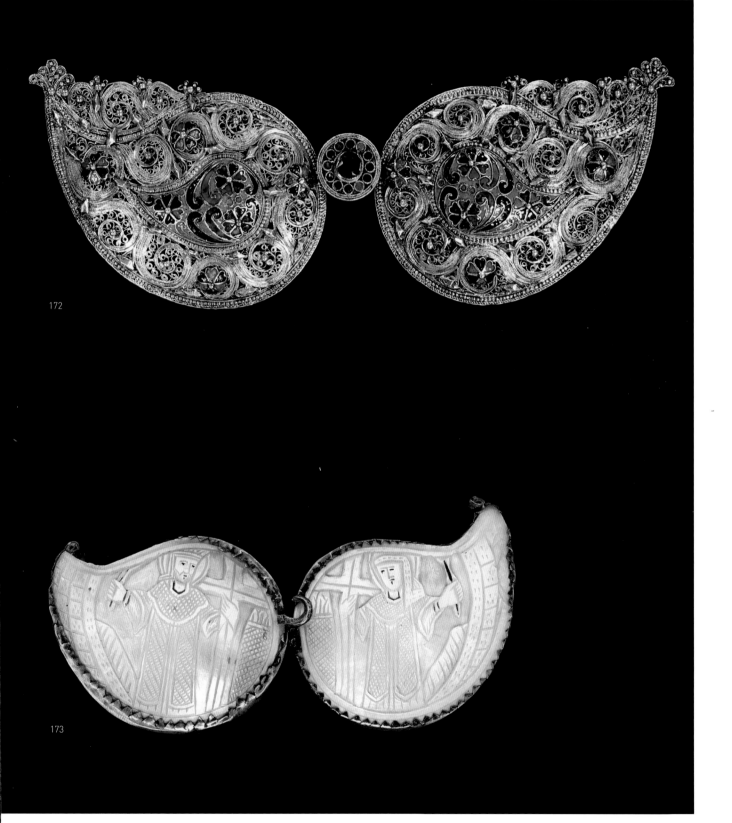

172

173

was made by specialists in a limited number of places, such as Yiannina in northern Greece, Dubrovnik on the Dalmatian coast of Croatia and Vratsa in Bulgaria. Clasps set with coral, particularly striated inlays, were a speciality of Saphrampolis (now Safranbolu in Turkey) (plate 171). They were objects of great refinement, which were traded throughout the Balkans. Those, usually comma-shaped, with carved mother-of-pearl plaques, are almost always Christian (plate 173). The plaques mainly came from the Holy Land, where their production was an important industry based in Bethlehem and Jerusalem; they are also sometimes ascribed to Mount Athos. Cyprus was a centre for fine filigree and enamel, usually in shades of blue and green (plate 172). Smaller clasps of similar shape were used to fasten the waistcoat or jacket, often several at a time. These were hooked into the costume when worn, rather than sewn permanently to a particular garment.

Although often belted, men's costumes rarely included decorative buckles or clasps, which would have impeded the easy use of the weapons worn thrust into their sashes (see plate 7). However large and heavy, Balkan clasps were always worn by women. The only men who wore belt clasps were the higher orders of the Orthodox Church.

Chains

One of the main characteristics of traditional jewellery in eastern Europe is the lavish use of chains. This is most pronounced in Russia, where chains, along with buttons and earrings, are the most distinctive elements of local jewellery

174　　**Russian chains**
　　A　Silver, length
　　　　71cm, 1850–1900.
　　　　Private collection;
　　B　Silver, length
　　　　99.4cm, 1750–1850.
　　　　V&A: 148–1906;
　　C　Silver-gilt and enamel,
　　　　length 88.1cm, 1850–80.
　　　　V&A: 159–1889;
　　D　Silver-gilt, length
　　　　105cm, 1650–1700.
　　　　Private collection;
　　E　White metal, length
　　　　154cm, 1850–1900.
　　　　Private collection
　　F　Silver-gilt, length
　　　　97cm, 1750–1800.
　　　　Private collection;

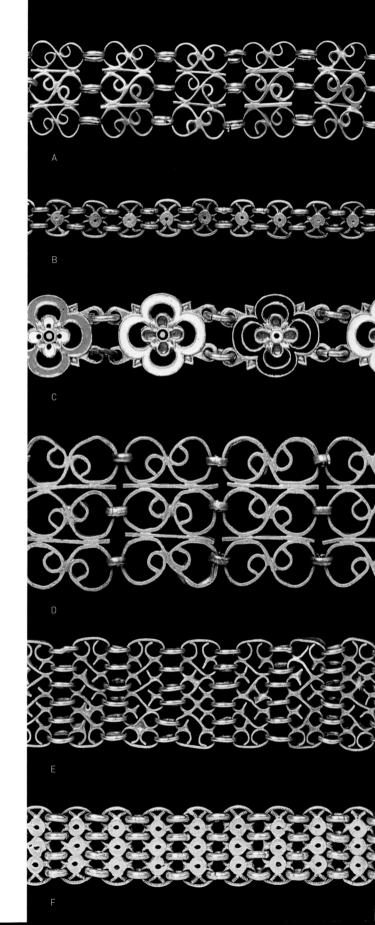

A

B

C

D

E

F

(plate 174). Russian traditional chains are very long, and usually made of decorative links of filigree scrolls, sometimes as many as five across. They were worn by both men and women from the seventeenth century onwards. By the nineteenth century their use was largely restricted to the conservative rural population and religious orders. They were worn universally by priests, usually several at a time, to carry crosses and religious pendants, and are sometimes known as priests' chains as a result. Lay people wore them in large quantities, sometimes strung in festoons round the neck (plate 175), or sewn on a cloth backing and worn diagonally across the shoulder, like a baldric. Although they originated in European Russia, they were widely worn throughout the Russian Empire by all faiths, and can be found in use as far south as the Balkans.

Balkan chains are less elaborate than those worn in Russia, and achieve their effect more by the way that they are worn than by the complexity of the links. Men wore thick watch chains of woven wire (plate 176), hooked into their jacket at the shoulder. In Cyprus the chain supported a circular box, resembling a watch or amulet case, which was used to contain all kinds of personal objects (plate 178). The fighters in the Greek War of Independence wore crossed chains on their chest, decorated with plaques of niello work celebrating their struggle. These crossed chains were also worn by women, particularly the seasonal Karagouna (see plate 1) and Sarakatsani transhumance herders (plate 177).

175 **Estonian woman, early
      20th century**
      Russian Museum of
      Ethnography

This young woman from
Estonia is wearing a mix
of Baltic and Russian
traditional jewellery.
The most obvious is the
mass of Russian filigree
chains, many with coins
and other pendants.
Under them it is just
possible to see some ring
brooches (see chapter 1).

176 Watch chain

Silver filigree set with
imitation amber, coral and
a green paste, length 62cm.
Dalmatia, Croatia,
1800–1900.
Private collection

This chain was worn by
men, hooked onto the
shoulder, with a watch
attached to the lower end
tucked into the sash. The
loose strap at the bottom
would have held watch keys
or other pendants. Similar
chains were worn
in Albania.

Women's chains were worn across the breast (plate 179), round the waist and in loops over the apron in Greece and Bulgaria, and in multiple strands under the chin, and round the wrist. Many of these chains have pendants attached, such as leaves or coins, which would have had an amuletic purpose. Chains were also used to link other elements of jewellery, and acted as necklaces everywhere. The preference for chains is widespread throughout the Balkans and Russia, and may be eastern in origin. It contrasts strongly with the central European love of beaded necklaces, which extends into parts of Croatia and Romania.

Religious pendants and amulets

Throughout the region, people wore amulets and religious symbols to help protect them from all kinds of danger as much as to proclaim their religious identity. In the Balkans everyone, especially women and children who were felt to be particularly vulnerable, wore amulet cases. These often contained religious texts, pieces of cloth, or other material of special significance, but the shape alone was considered sufficient to be effective.

In many cases, there was little difference in the shapes worn by different faiths. Triangular and cylindrical amulet cases are probably Islamic in origin, while the round, flat version was more common among Orthodox Christians. Rectangular amulet cases were generally worn by men (plate 181). The decoration varied by faith. Muslim amulet cases have calligraphic or floral designs, while Christian cases usually have religious motifs, but not all symbols are as obvious in meaning as might be

177 **Kiousteki from Thessaly**
From *Kosmēmata tēs Hellēnikēs paradosiakēs phoresias, 1800s-1900s*, Ethnikou Historikou Mouseiou (Athens, 1995)

Kiousteki were elegant arrangements of chains worn on the body and over the skirt in northern Greece. They were mainly worn by women, but men also wore them in the 1820s, during the Greek War of Independence.

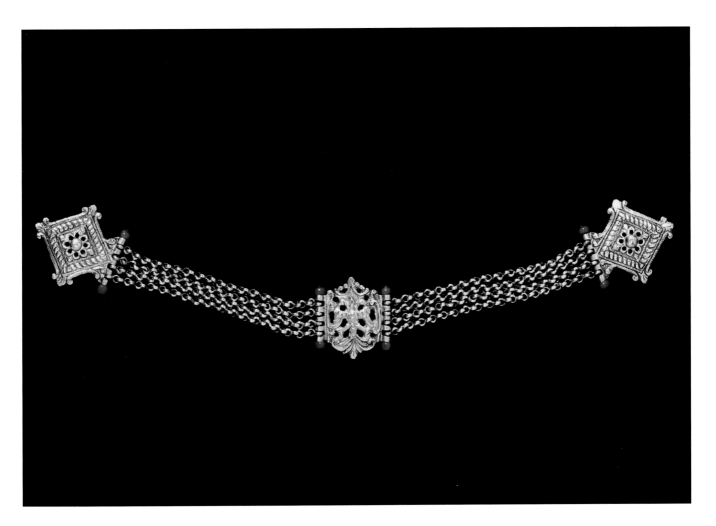

178 **Case (*Ambousta tou korfou*) with chain**
Silver with niello, filigree and a blue paste, diam. 4.7cm (case). Cyprus, 1750–1850.
V&A: 1548–1888

The shape of this case is based on an Ottoman watch case. It was worn by a man, and may have contained a watch, but was also used for all kinds of other small personal items, such as tobacco or coins. The name is derived from an Italian word for a pouch.

179 **Chain**
Silver with red glass beads, length 31.5cm. Epirus, northwest Greece, 1860–70.
V&A: 1436–1873

This chain was worn by a woman to fasten the sides of her waistcoat or jacket together. The double-headed eagle was a very common symbol throughout the Balkans, and was used by all communities to express power.

180 Clasp
Silver and copper, width
38cm. Greece or Bulgaria,
1800–70.
Private collection

Large sheet silver clasps
are mainly found in northern
Greece and Bulgaria. The
tree of life on the central
part, and the birds on
the sides, emphasize the
amuletic purpose of the
belt, to promote fertility and
avert any danger to unborn
children. The bars on the
back are made of copper.

181 Amulet case
Silver, width 8.5cm.
Greece or Albania, c.1860.
V&A: 1421–1873

This amulet case has
the repoussé figure of
St George, the patron saint
of Greece, on the front.
Amulet cases like this were
usually worn by men.

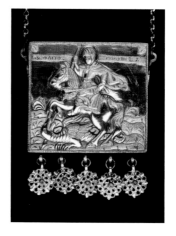

182 **Cross pendant**
Cast silver, length 4.6cm.
Russia, 1800–60.
V&A: 109–1866

183 **Cross pendant**
Cast silver, length 6.9cm.
Russia, 1800–60.
V&A: 510–1869

184 **Cross pendant**
Cast silver, length 7.2cm.
Russia, 1800–60.
V&A: 110–1866

185 **Cross pendant**
Silver and enamel, length
5.8cm. Russia, 1800–60.
V&A: 106–1866

These crosses incorporate
elements of Russian
Orthodox iconography,
including a *tsata*, or collar,
at the centre and an oblique
bar just above the foot. Plate
184 has the lance and the
sponge of the Crucifixion at
either side of the upright,
almost hidden by a mass
of pierced foliage and
rosettes. There are letters
in Cyrillic script along the
ends of the arms. They were
all probably made in the
nineteenth century, but the
same designs have been
used for centuries and are
still being made today.

thought. Many were used by members of all three Abrahamic religions, such as the tree of life, various unidentifiable birds, alternately described as eagles, doves or cockerels (plate 180), and the six-pointed Star of David. Only the cross, and images of saints and churches, were unique to Christians.

The religious devotion of the Russian peasantry was legendary, and everyone would have owned a pendent cross. Russian crosses are usually orthodox in form, with a sloping bar across the lower part, and lettering in Cyrillic characters (plate 182). The basic cross is often surrounded by an elaborate pierced frame (plates 183 and 184). The revival of Russian nationalism at the end of the nineteenth century led to a renewed interest in traditional kinds of metalwork, including enamel (plate 185), niello and filigree. The designs of traditional chains and pendants (plate 186) became fashionable then not only among richer urban Russians, but also in western Europe, as part of the general interest in 'peasant' jewellery.

In the Balkans, crosses were often simpler, and more similar to those worn in Catholic Europe. Hollow pendent reliquary crosses, which could be opened to contain a relic, were common, as were elaborate filigree designs, usually hung from heavy chains of hand-made figure-of-eight links. Despite its name, the so-called Greek cross, with arms of equal length, is rarely found as a pendant in Greek traditional jewellery.

Bracelets

The Balkans is the only region in Europe where bracelets form part of the traditional jewellery. Everywhere else they are either

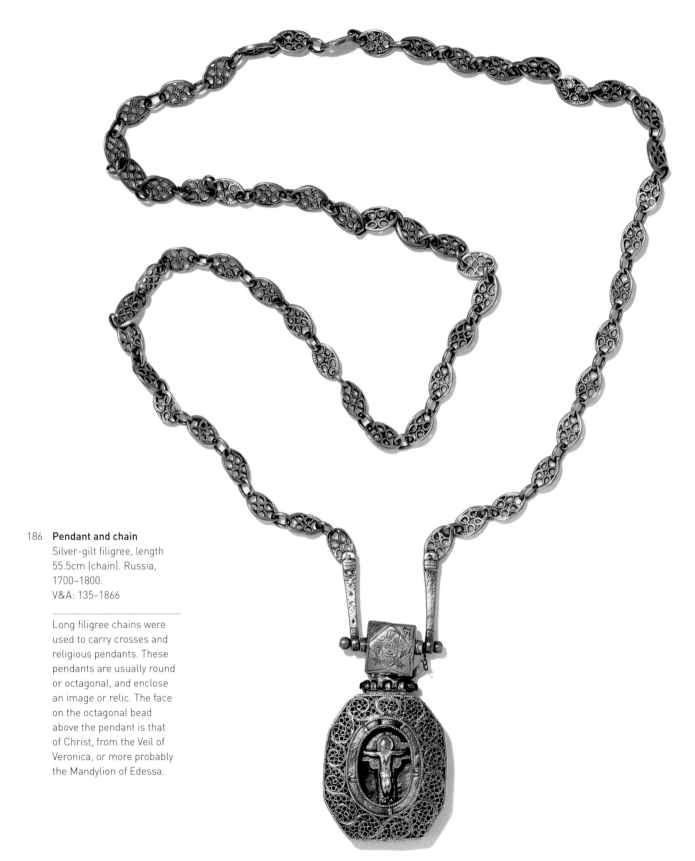

186 Pendant and chain
Silver-gilt filigree, length
55.5cm (chain). Russia,
1700–1800.
V&A: 135–1866

Long filigree chains were
used to carry crosses and
religious pendants. These
pendants are usually round
or octagonal, and enclose
an image or relic. The face
on the octagonal bead
above the pendant is that
of Christ, from the Veil of
Veronica, or more probably
the Mandylion of Edessa.

entirely non-existent, or first make their appearance in the late nineteenth century, to match existing items of jewellery. Their use in the Balkans may be Ottoman in origin. Bracelets were widely worn in the region to the end of the Byzantine Empire, and were sometimes used as a symbol of office for men, but they never entered popular tradition, and are entirely absent from Russian traditional jewellery. Under the Ottoman Empire, bracelets were a well-established part of the Moslem wedding tradition: the mother-in-law placed a pair on the bride's wrists on her henna night.

The oldest types of bracelet in the Balkans are penannular, cast in heavy bronze alloy. They come mainly from Thrace, and intermediate examples in the National History Museum in Sofia suggest a direct descent from a Slav original. The shape of the protrusions, resembling women's breasts, inevitably led to associations with fertility and child-bearing. Hinged bracelets, of the kind worn throughout Europe in the nineteenth century, are found in many places in eastern Europe, but chain bracelets, of several strands linking two decorative ends, or a single complex strap, are Ottoman in origin, and can be found throughout the countries of the eastern Mediterranean.

Buttons

Buttons were one of the few items of jewellery allowed to men. In the sixteenth and seventeenth centuries, spherical or oval decorative buttons were worn in large numbers by all ranks of society in Russia. These traditional ovoid buttons largely went out of fashion among the aristocracy, along with most other aspects of traditional costume, in the eighteenth century. They remained important for the conservative rural population, however, until the Russian Revolution, particularly those made of filigree. These were sometimes worn on men's costume, but by the nineteenth century more commonly by women, as pendants hung from chains. In the Balkans, most decorative buttons were made of bullion thread, in the Ottoman tradition, rather than precious metals, and were worn lavishly, by both sexes, on all their outer garments. In a few places, such as Konavle in Croatia, these thread buttons were replaced by silver filigree on women's bridal dress, and were an essential part of the dowry. The large silver filigree buttons worn by men in Dalmatia and Albania (plate 187) may have been based on the buttons traditionally worn by the Doge of Venice, the overlord of much of the coastal region before the nineteenth century.

187 **Toggle button**
Silver filigree, length 5cm.
Dalmatia, 1800–1900.
V&A: CIRC.20–1951

Toggle buttons were worn by men to fasten their waistcoats and jackets; the toggle fitting saved them from having to be sewn permanently to one garment. Dalmatian filigree toggle buttons are probably Italian in origin.

Further information

This book can only be an introduction to the vast and fascinating subject of traditional jewellery in Europe. Most of the pieces illustrated are in the collections of the V&A, and further, more detailed, information about each of them, including full measurements and information about the maker where known, can be found on the V&A website, at www.vam.ac.uk, in 'Search the Collections'. The majority of these pieces can also be seen on display in the William and Judith Bollinger Jewellery Gallery, and all these have images available on the website. If a maker's name is not listed in the caption, it is not known.

The bibliography lists sources for information about individual countries, and these books will usually provide names of appropriate regional museums. A full list of European museums with jewellery in their collections can be found on the website of The Society of Jewellery Historians, at www.societyofjewelleryhistorians.ac.uk/museums_Europe.

Acknowledgements

I am glad of this opportunity to acknowledge the great debt I owe to Richard Edgcumbe, without whom this book would not have existed and who has supported and encouraged me throughout, and to Beatriz Chadour-Sampson, who has been indefatigable in making useful suggestions and amendments. I am also grateful for the help and advice I have received from other scholars and colleagues, including Frances Ambler, Marian Campbell, Jane Sconce and Joanne Whalley at the V&A, Judy Rudoe at the British Museum, Antonia Herradon, Claudette Joannis, Lia Lenti, Francesco Polizzi, Vivianne Veenemans and Muriel Wilson.

Nordic and central Europe

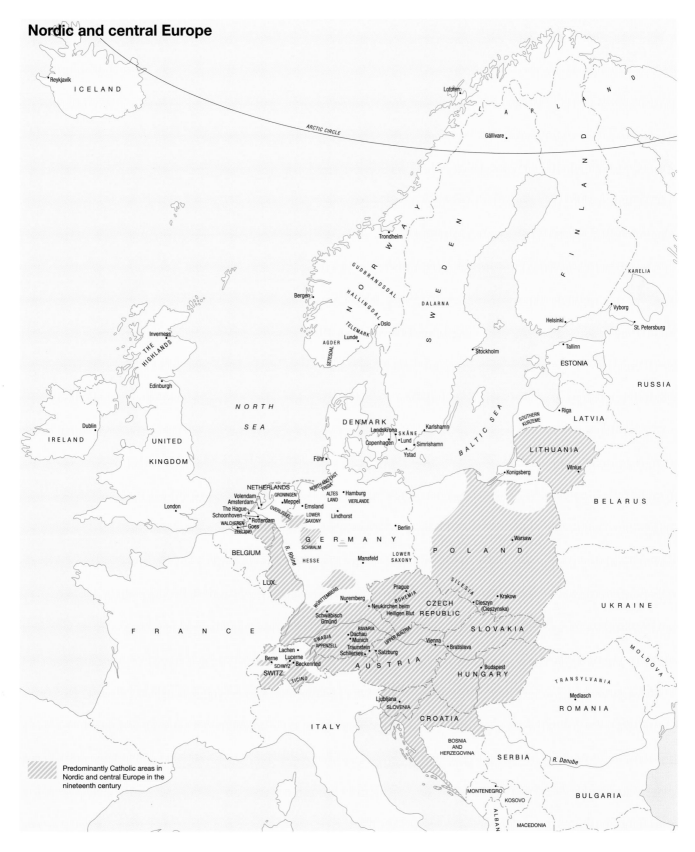

ICELAND
• Reykjavik

ARCTIC CIRCLE

• Lofoten

L A P L A N D

• Gällivare

THE HIGHLANDS
• Inverness

• Trondheim

N O R W A Y

GUDBRANDSDAL

HALLINGDAL

• Bergen

TELEMARK
• Oslo
• Lunde

AGDER

SETESDAL

S W E D E N

DALARNA

F I N L A N D

KARELIA

• Helsinki
• Vyborg
• St. Petersburg

• Edinburgh

NORTH SEA

• Stockholm

• Tallinn

ESTONIA

R U S S I A

IRELAND
• Dublin

UNITED KINGDOM

DENMARK

• Landskrona
SKÅNE
Copenhagen •
• Lund • Simrishamn
• Ystad
• Karlshamn

BALTIC SEA

SOUTHERN KURZEME

• Riga

LATVIA

B E L A R U S

• London

• Föhr

NETHERLANDS
Volendam •
Amsterdam •
The Hague •
Schoonhoven •
Rotterdam •
WALCHEREN • Goes
ZEELAND

GRONINGEN
Meppel •

OVERIJSSEL

NORTH AND EAST FRISIA

ALTES LAND
• Hamburg
VIERLANDE

• Emsland

LOWER SAXONY
• Lindhorst

LITHUANIA
• Vilnius

• Königsberg

• Berlin

• Warsaw

P O L A N D

BELGIUM

SCHWALM

G E R M A N Y

HESSE

• Mansfeld

LOWER SAXONY

SILESIA

• Krakow
Cieszyn •
(Cieszynska)

U K R A I N E

LUX.

R. Rhine

WÜRTTEMBERG

• Nuremberg

Prague •

BOHEMIA

• Neukirchen beim
Heiligen Blut

CZECH REPUBLIC

SLOVAKIA

MOLDOVA

F R A N C E

Schwäbisch
Gmünd •

SWABIA
APPENZELL

BAVARIA
• Dachau
• Munich
• Traunstein
Schliersee •

UPPER AUSTRIA

• Salzburg

A U S T R I A

• Vienna • Bratislava

H U N G A R Y
• Budapest

TRANSYLVANIA
• Mediasch

R O M A N I A

Lachen •
Berne • • Lucerne
SCHWYZ • Beckenried
SWITZ.
TICINO

• Ljubljana
SLOVENIA

I T A L Y

CROATIA

BOSNIA AND HERZEGOVINA

SERBIA

R. Danube

MONTENEGRO

KOSOVO

ALBAN.

MACEDONIA

B U L G A R I A

Santiago de Compostela
•

GALICIA

Astorga
•

LEÓN

• Zamora

•Oporto

• Salamanc

• La Alberca

P
O
R
T
U
G
A
L

EXTREMADURA

•Lisbon

S P A

I
B
E
R
I
A

Cordoba
•

Seville
•

A N D A L U S I A

MA

M O R O C C O

BELGIUM

GERMANY

Boulogne-
sur-Mer

Saint-Lô

NORMANDY

Yvetot
Rouen

Amiens

BRITTANY

CZECH REPUBLIC

Guibray

Alençon

Paris

R. Rhine

VENDÉE

BURGUNDY

ALSACE

R. Danube

FRANCE

AUSTRIA

Niort

POITOU

Mâcon

Bourg-en-
Bresse

SWITZERLAND

SLOVENIA

AUVERGNE

SAVOY

BRIANZA

Bourg-
Saint-
Maurice

Oropa

LOMBARDY

Novara

Milan

Venice

Turin

PROVENCE

PIEDMONT

CROATIA

Beaucaire

ROMAGNA

BOSNIA
AND
HERZEGOVINA

Saragossa

TUSCANY

Sant'Angelo in Vado

CATALONIA

Loreto

ITALY

MARCHE

STILE

PAPAL
STATES

Scanno

Barcelona

Rome

ABRUZZO

MOLISE

VALENCIA

Frosolone

Bovino

MURCIA

Pozzuoli

APULIA

Naples

Nuoro

SARDINIA

Cagliari

Palermo

Piana degli
Albanesi

SICILY

TUNISIA

MALTA

Valletta

LIBYA

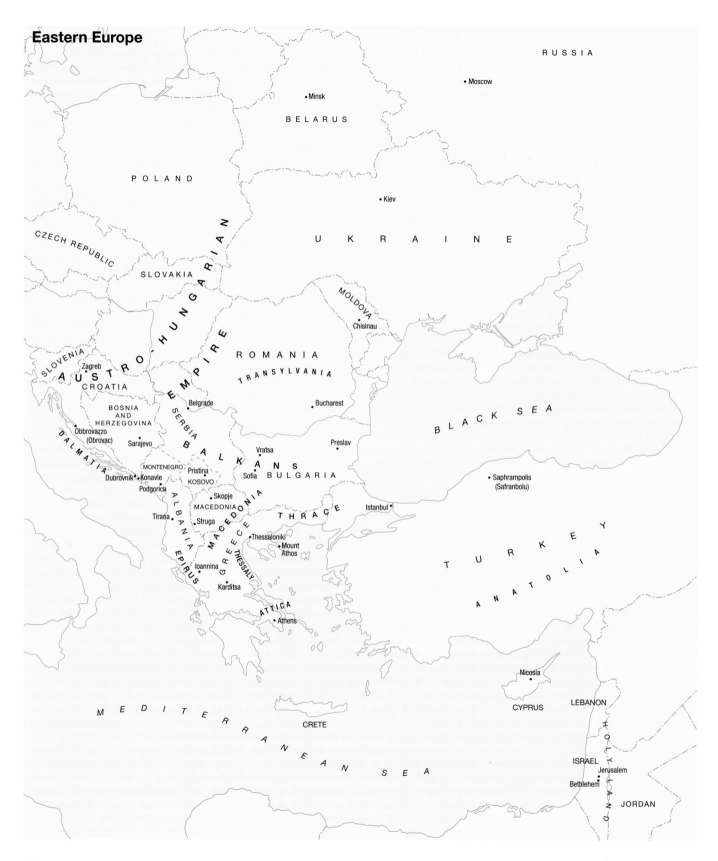

Eastern Europe

RUSSIA

• Moscow

• Minsk

BELARUS

POLAND

• Kiev

CZECH REPUBLIC

U K R A I N E

SLOVAKIA

AUSTRO-HUNGARIAN EMPIRE

MOLDOVA

• Chisinau

SLOVENIA

Zagreb

ROMANIA

CROATIA

TRANSYLVANIA

BOSNIA
AND
HERZEGOVINA

SERBIA

• Belgrade

• Bucharest

BLACK SEA

Obbrovazzo
(Obrovac)

DALMATIA

• Sarajevo

B A L K A N S

Vratsa

• Preslav

MONTENEGRO

Pristina

Dubrovnik

Konavle

KOSOVO

• Sofia

BULGARIA

Saphrampolis
(Safranbolu)

Podgorica

• Skopje

ALBANIA

MACEDONIA

THRACE

Istanbul •

Tirana

• Struga

MACEDONIA

T U R K E Y

EPIRUS

GREECE

THESSALY

• Thessaloniki

• Ioannina

• Mount
Athos

ANATOLIA

• Karditsa

ATTICA

• Athens

• Nicosia

M E D I T E R R A N E A N   S E A

CYPRUS

LEBANON

CRETE

HOLY LAND

ISRAEL

Jerusalem

• Bethlehem

JORDAN

Chadour, B. and Joppien, R., *Schmuck. Kataloge des Kunstgewerbemuseums Köln, Band X, 2 vols* (Cologne, 1985)

Fredrickson, N. Jaye, *The Covenant Chain: Indian Ceremonial and Trade Silver* (Canada, 1980)

Gere, C. and Rudoe, J., *Jewellery in the Age of Queen Victoria: A Mirror to the World* (London, 2010)

Gerlach, Martin (ed.), *Primitive and Folk Jewellery* (An English translation of '*Völkerschmuck*' by Dr. M. Haberlandt) (New York, 1971)

Göbel, Karin et al., *Auf's Ohr geschaut. Ohrringe aus Stadt und Land vom Klassizismus bis zur Neuen Jugendkultur* (Berlin, 1989)

Haberlandt, Dr. M., *Völkerschmuck* (Vienna/Leipzig, 1906)

Hinks, Peter, *Nineteenth Century Jewellery* (London, 1975)

Jargstorf, Sibylle, *Ethnic Jewelry from Africa, Europe and Asia* (USA, 2007)

Musée de la Vie Wallonne, *Love and Marriage. Aspects of Folk-life in Europe* (Liège, 1975)

Percival, MacIver, *Chats on old Jewellery and Trinkets* (London, 1912)

Perry, Jane, *A Collector's Guide to Peasant Silver Buttons* (Lulu.com, 2007)

Perry, Jane, 'The Victorian Passion for Peasant Jewellery', *Jewellery Studies*, vol.12 (2012)

Van Nespen, W., *Love and Marriage. Aspects of Popular Culture in Europe* (Antwerp, 1975)

Denmark

Schoubye, Sigurd, *Guldsmede-Håndvaerket i Tønder of pä Tønder-Egnen 1550–1900* (Aarhus, 1961)

Estonia

Kirme, Kaalu, *Eesti Rahvapärased Ehted: 13. sajand–20. sajandi algus* (Estonia, 2002)

Kirme, Kaalu, *Eesti Soled* (Tallinn, Estonia, 1986)

Iceland

Magnusson, Thor, *Silfur i Thjodminjasafni* (Reykjavik, 1996)

Lapland

Fjellström Phebe, *Lapskt Silver* (Stockholm, 1962)

Lithuania

Kulikauskiene, R., *Lietuviu Liadies Menas: Papuosalai* (Vilnius, Lithuania, 1958)

Norway

Berge, Rikard, *Norskt Bondesylv* (Oslo, 1925; reprinted 1975)

Fossberg, Jorunn, *Draktsølv* (Oslo, 1991)

Noss, Aagot, *Lad og Krone: frå Jente til Brur* (Norway, 1991)

Noss, Aagot, *Sylvsmeden Eivind G Tveiten* (Oslo, 1970)

Skauhaug, Kjersti, *Norwegian Bunads* (Oslo, 1989)

Scotland

Marshall, R.K. and Dalgliesh, G.R., *The Art of Jewellery in Scotland* (Edinburgh, 1991)

National Museum, *Brooches in Scotland* (Edinburgh, 1958)

Sweden

Hovstadius, Barbro, *Brudkronor i Linköpings Stift* (Stockholm, 1976)

Plath, Iona, *The Decorative Arts of Sweden* (USA, 1966)

Svensson, Sigfrid, *Folkligt Dräktsilver* (Västerås, 1978)

de Bree, J., *Kostuum en Sieraad in Zeeland* (Arnhem, 1985)

Jansen, B. et al., *Het Gouden Sieraad in de Nederlandse Folklore* ('s-Gravenhage, 1955)

Leopold, J.H., *Goud en zilver van het Groninger Land. Groninger Streekdrachtsieraden 1800–1900* (Groningen, 1984)

Minderhoud, P.J., *Van De Goudsmid. De historie en de Ontwikkeling van Zeeuwse en Andere Streeksieraden* (Enschede, 2010)

Museum Boymans-van Beuningen, *Boerenpracht en Visserstooi. Klederdrachtsieraden in Nederland* (Rotterdam, 1975)

Nederlands Goud-, Zilver- en Klokkenmuseum, *Drie Eeuwen Schoonhovens Zilver* (Schoonhoven, 1981)

Nieuwhoff, Constance, *The Costumes of Holland* (Amsterdam, 1985)

Wttewaall, B.W.G., *Nederlands Klein Zilver en Schepwerk 1650–1880* (Abcoude, 1994; updated 2003)

Bibliography

3 Central Europe

Austria
Hempel, Gudrun, *Schmuck – Filigrane Kunst aus Gold- und Silberfäden* (Vienna, 1995)
Hempel, Gudrun, *Zumachen – Aufmachen* (Vienna, 1983)
Nemec, H., *Alter Bauernschmuck* (Vienna/Munich, 1973)

Czech Republic
Dembiniok, Marian, *Krojové Stříbtné Šperky Těšínského Slezska* (Těšin, Czech Republic, 2000)

Germany
Behrmann, Inge (ed.), *Volkstümlicher Schmuck. Kataloge des Museums für Kunst und Gewerbe Hamburg, Band VII* (Hamburg, 1985)
Behrmann, I. and Küster, C.L., *Volkstümlicher Schmuck aus Norddeutschland* (Hamburg, 1979)
Deneke, Bernward, *Volkstümlicher Schmuck aus Nordwestdeutschland* (Leer, 1977)
Ergert, Bernd, *Jagd- und Trachtenschmuck* (Munich, 1978)
Gierl, Irmgard, *Trachtenschmuck aus fünf Jahrhunderten* (Rosenheim, 1972)
Klein, Walter, *Sechshundert Jahre Gmünder Goldschmiedekunst* (Stuttgart, 1947)
Krause-Schmidt, Heike, *ihr Brodt mit kleiner Silber-Arbeit erwerben* (Schwäbisch Gmünd, 1999)
Röhrs, Ursula, *Alter Volkstümlicher Fingerschmuck* (Schwäbisch-Gmünd, 1999)
Röhrs, Ursula, *Der Ring – 50 Jahre Schmuck, Magie, Handwerk und Design* (Schwäbisch-Gmünd, 2011)
Scherer, Peter (ed.), *Das Gmünder Schmuckhandwerk bis zum Beginn des XIX. Jahrhunderts* (Schwäbisch Gmünd, 1971)
Schmuckmuseum Pforzheim, *Schmuck zum Gwand. Ländliche Bijouteriewaren aus dem Bayerischen Nationalmuseum München* (Pforzheim, 2010)
Stierling, Hubert, *Der Silberschmuck der Nordseeküste. I. Bd.: Geschichtliche Entwicklung seit dem Mittelalter* (Neumünster, 1935; reprinted 2000)

Wiswe, Mechthild, *Volkstümlicher Schmuck aus dem Braunschweigischen* (Braunschweig, 1977)

German-speaking region
Bott, Gerhard (ed.), *Ländlicher Schmuck aus Deutschland, Österreich und der Schweiz* (Nuremberg, 1982)
Holme, Charles (ed.), *Peasant Art in Austria and Hungary* (London, 1911)
Maue, H. and Veit, L. (eds), *Münzen in Brauch und Aberglauben* (Mainz, 1982)
Ritz, Gislind, *Alter Bäuerlicher Schmuck* (Munich, 1978)

Hungary
Balogh-Horváth, Terézia, *Hungarian Folk Jewelry* (Budapest, 1983)
Héjj-Détári, Angéla, *Hungarian Jewellery of the Past* (Budapest, 1976)
Kovács, Tibor, *Török Ékszerek* (Hungary, undated)

Poland
Koszutska, Jadwiga, *Hoczki cieszyńskie* (Warsaw, 1985)
Michalczyk, Maria, *Hoczki, Knefle, Orpanty... Biżuteria Cieszyńska w Zbiorach* (Katowice, 2007)
Piskorz-Branekova, Elżbieta, *Biżuteria Ludowa w Polsce* (Warsaw, 2008)
Seweryn, Tadeusz, *Krakowskie klejnoty ludowe* (Krakow, 1935)

Slovakia
Johnova, Helena, *Schmuck* (Bratislava, 1986)

Slovenia
Žagar, Janja, *Pasovi in sklepanci* (Ljubljana, 1993)

Switzerland
Baud-Bovy, Daniel, *Peasant Art in Switzerland* (London, 1924)
Chadour-Sampson, Beatriz, *Trachtenbilder und Deli in der Sammlung Dr. Edmund Müller* (Beromünster, 2002)
Rusch, Carl, *Der Appenzell-Innerrhodische Trachtenschmuck* (Appenzell, 1974)
Schneider, Dr. Jenny, *Schweizer Trachtenschmuck* (Bern, 1965)

4 France

Bouret, Brigitte, *Bijoux et Orfèvres en Haute Normandie* (Normandy, 1993)
Bruneau, M., *Les Bijoux Normandes* (Rouen, 1974)
Bruno, Agnes, *Emaux Bressans, Parures Charmantes* (Bourg-en-Bresse, 1992)
Cuisenier, Jean (ed.), *Costume Coutume: Galeries Nationales du Grand Palais, 16 Mars–15 Juin 1987* (Paris, 1987)
Gendron, Christian, *Les Bijoux Traditionnels Poitevins; Catalogue des Collections Publiques du Poitou-Vendée* (Niort, 1992)
Joannis, Claudette, *Bijoux des Régions de France* (Paris, 1992)
Kertenian, Remy, *Le Bijou Provençal: Parures du Quotidien et Bijoux de Fête* (Geneva, 2003)
Poulenc, M. and Margerie, A-M., *Les Bijoux Traditionnels Français* (Paris, 1998)
Trosset, Jean-Pierre, *Bijoux et Croix des Provinces de Savoie* (Bresson, 2003)

5 Italy   ## 6 Spain and Portugal   ## 7 The Eastern Frontier

Ashbee, C.R., *The Treatises of Benvenuto Cellini on Goldsmithing and Sculpture (Translated from the Italian)* (London, 1888; reprinted New York, 1967)
Arundel Society, *Italian Jewellery as worn by the Peasants of Italy. Collected by Signor Castellani, and purchased from the Paris Universal Exhibition for the South Kensington Museum* (London, 1868)
Cavalcanti, Ottavio, *Ori e Argenti del Sud – Gioielli in Basilicata* (Matera, 1996)
Cavalcanti, Ottavio, *Ori Antichi di Calabria* (Palermo, 1991)
Clemente, Pietro et al., *Gioielli. Storia, Linguaggio, Religiosità dell'Ornamento in Sardegna* (Nuoro, 2004)
de Luca, Stefano (ed.), *L'Ornamento Prezioso* (Rome, 1986)
Frohlich, R. and M., *Filigran aus Cortina d'Ampezzo um die Jahrhundertwende* (Zurich, 1980)
Gandolfi, A. and Mattiocco, E. (eds), *Ori e Argenti d'Abruzzo dal Medioevo al XX Secolo* (Pescara, 1996)
Gandolfo, F. and Lenti, L., *Gioielli. Collezioni Etnografiche Subalpine* (Turin, 2004)
Gometz, Piergiorgio, *Gioielli di Sardegna: Tradizione, Arte, Magia* (Cagliari, 1995)
Gri, G.P. and Cantarutti, N., *La Collezione Perusini. Ori, Gioielli e Amuleti Tradizionali* (Udine, 1988)
Holme, Charles (ed.), *Peasant Art in Italy* (London, 1913)
Lenti, Lia, *La Tradizione Preciosa. Filigrane Vercellesi al Museo Leone* (Vercelli, 2007)
Museo Civico di Belluno, *Ori del Costume Bellunese* (Belluno, 1986)
Museo Nazionale delle Arti e Tradizioni Popolari, *I Modelli del Tempo* (Rome, 2001)
Pesce, G., *Filigrana Ieri ed Oggi* (Genova, 1973)
Pisani, D., *Il Gioiello Popolare Calabrese* (Naples, 1997)
Rossi, Annabella, **Oreficeria Popolare Italiana** (Rome, 1984)
Spina, L. (ed.), *Orafi e Ori. Cultura Materiale nel Biellese* (Biella, 1996)
Tripputi, A.M. and Mavelli, R., *Ori del Gargano* (Foggia, 2005)

Portugal
Costa, A. and de Freitas, R.M., *Ouro Popular Português* (Porto, 1992)
de Vasconcelos e Sousa, Dr. Gonçalo, *A Joalharia em Portugal 1750–1825* (Porto, 2006)
D'Orey, Leonor, *Five Centuries of Jewellery; National Museum of Ancient Art, Lisbon* (London, 1995)
Guedes, Rui, *Joalharia Portuguesa: Portuguese Jewellery* (Lisbon, 1995)
Macedo, Fatima, *Raizes do Ouro Popular do Noroeste Português* (Porto, 1993)
Rosas (junior), José, *Jóias Portuguesas: as 'Laças de Ouro'* (Porto, 1942)

Spain
Castellano Caja de Ahorros, *Joyería Popular de Zamora* (Zamora, 1985)
Pérez, O.C. and González, J.A., *Indumentaria y Joyería Tradicional de La Bañeza y su Comarca* (León, 2002)
Herradon Figueroa, Maria Antonia, *La Alberca Joyas* (Madrid, 2005)
Muller, Priscilla E., *Jewels in Spain, 1500–1800* (New York, 1972; updated 2012)
Museu del Pueblo Espanol, *Catalogo de Amuletos* (Madrid, 1987)
Museu del Pueblo Espanol, *Joyas Populares* (Madrid, 1984)
Sanchez, Carlos Pinel, *La Belleza que Protégé* (Spain, 1998)

Bosnia
Horniman Museum, **Folk Embroidery and Jewellery of Bosnia-Herzegovina** (London, 1975)

Bulgaria
Blagoeva, Snejana, **Bulgarian Jewellery** (Sofia, 1977)
Blagoeva, Snejana, *Bulgarsky Pafti i Kolani/Bulgarian Buckles and Belts* (Sofia, undated)
Drumev, Dimitar, *Zlatarsko Iskustvo/ Orfèvrerie* (Sofia, 1976)
Georgieva, S. and Buchinsky, D., *Staroto Zlatarstvo vv Vratsa* (Sofia, 1959)
Sotirov, Ivan, *Chiprovska Zlatarska Shkola* (Sofia, 1976)
Veleva, M. and Dancheva-Blagoeva, S., *Bulgarian National Costumes and Folk Jewellery* (Sofia, 1983)

Croatia
Bruck-Auffenberg, Natalie, *Dalmatien und seine Volkskunst* (Vienna/Paris, 1912)
Vrtovec, Ivanka, *Croatian National Jewelry* (Zagreb, 1985)

Cyprus
Rizopoulou-Egoumenidou, Efrosini, *I Astiki Endumasia tis Kyprou* (Nicosia, 1996)

Greece
Bromberg, Anne R., *Gold of Greece: Jewelry and Ornaments from the Benaki Museum* (Dallas, 1990)
Delivorrias, Angelos, *Greek Traditional Jewelry* (Athens, 1979)
Hagimihali, Angélique, *L'Art Populaire Grec* (Athens, 1937)
Hatzimichali, Angeliki, *The Greek Folk Costume* (Greece, 1977)
Historical & Ethnological Society of Greece, *Greek costumes* (Athens, 1993)
Historical & Ethnological Society of Greece, *Kosmimata tis Ellinikis Paradosiakis Foresias 1800–1900* (Athens, 1995)

Kypraiou, Evangelia, *Greek Jewellery: 6,000 years of Tradition* (Athens, 1997)
Thessalonica, City of, *The Goldsmiths of Nymphaion* (Thessalonica, 1995)
Zora, Popi, *Embroideries and Jewellery of Greek National Costumes* (Athens, 1966)

Russia
Dubow, Igor, et al., *Schatzkammer der Zarenvölker* (Pforzheim, 1991)
Medvedeva, G. et al., *Russian Jewellery 16th–20th Centuries, from the Collection of the Historical Museum, Moscow* (Moscow, 1987)
Postnikova-Loseva, M., *Iskusstvo Skani; The Art of Filigree* (Moscow, undated)
Postnikova-Loseva, M., *Russkaya Zolotaya i Serebryanaya Skan; Russian Gold and Silver Filigree* (Moscow, 1981)
Torchinskaya, E. et al., *Museum of the Ethnography of the Peoples of the USSR: Jewellery* (Leningrad, 1988)
Shatalovoi, I.V. (ed.), *Iuvelirnoe Iskusstvo Narodov Rossii/Jeweller's Art of the Peoples of Russia* (Leningrad, 1974)

Serbia
Belgrade, Ethnographic Museum, *Nakit i Kicenje* (Belgrade, 1971)
Branka, Ivanić, *Nakit iz zbirke Narodnog muzeja od 15. do pocetka 19. veka* (Belgrade, 1995)
Radojković, Bojana, *Nakit kod Srba od XII do kraja XVIII veka* (Belgrade, 1969)

Index

Page numbers in *italic* refer to
the illustrations

Abruzzo 83
Abruzzo 83, 95
Albania *16*
  amulets *130*
  belts and clasps *16, 82, 118,* 120
  buttons 133
  chains *130*
  earrings *118*
Altes Land 63, *63,* 67, *67*
Amagers 12
amber *8,* 38, 60
amethysts *18*
amulets 8
  Central Europe 64–5, *65*
  Eastern Europe, *130,* 128–31
  Italy 81, 85, 86–89, *88–90*
  Nordic region *8,* 37–8
  Spain and Portugal 107, *107*
Andalusia 108
Andersen, David 21
Appenzell 58
Arts and Crafts movement 19
Aspelin, J. the elder *29*
Astorga 99, *100, 104, 107*
Austria 51
  belts 67
  bodice fasteners 57
  brooches 63
  buttons 67
  hair ornaments 58
  necklaces and chains 34, 60, *60*
  ring brooches *12*
Auvergne 73

Balkans 8, 9, 113–14
  amulets 128
  belts and clasps 119–20, *122*
  bracelets 131–3
  buttons 133
  chains 126–8
  crosses 131
  earrings 116, *117–19*
  headdresses 114
  marriage jewellery 12
  silversmiths 11
Barcelona *99*
Bateman family 26
Bavaria 51, *57*
  amulets *65*
  bodice chains *57*
  buttons 67
  hair pins 58
  necklaces and chains 67
  rings 66, *66*
Belgium 41, 45, 71
belt hooks 78, *78*
belts: Central Europe *14, 18,* 66–7
  Eastern Europe 119
  Italy 81–2, *82*
  Nordic region 30–32, *33*
Bergen 28
Beul, F.L. *58*
Bleckberg, N. *36*
bodice fasteners
  Central Europe 54–8, *54–7*

Nordic region 27–8, *28–30*
Boers, J.M. *42*
Bosnia 116, *119*
Bourg-en-Bresse 78–9
bracelets 9, 14, 131–3
Bressan enamels 70, 78–9, *79*
Breton necklets 17, *17*
Brianza *81, 92*
bridal jewellery *see* marriage jewellery
Brittany 49, 69, 70
  crosses 73, *74*
brooches 9, *15*
  Central Europe *12,* 63–4, *64*
  France 77–8, *77*
  Nordic region 22–7, *22–7,* 37
buckles 30, 46, *46,* 67, 124
Bulgari, Sotirio 11
Bulgaria: chains 128
  clasps 124
  diadems 114, *114*
  earrings 116
Burgos *105*
buttons: Central Europe 52, 67, *67*
  Eastern Europe 113, 133, *133*
  Italy 95
  Netherlands 46–9, *46–9*
  Nordic region 38–9, *38–9*
  Spain and Portugal 111, *111*
Byzantine Empire 113, 114, 116, 120,
  133

Caccavallo, Antonio *84*
Calvinism 34, 41, 46–9
Catalonia 99
Catherine the Great, Empress 114
Catholic Church 41, 51, 54, 97
  amulets 52, 64
  crosses 45, 85
  earrings 14
  hair ornaments 58
  pendants 34
  rings 66
  rosaries 64–5
Cellini, Benvenuto 12, 83
Celtic jewellery 70, 97
Central America 97, 99–102
Central Europe 50–67
  amulets and religious jewellery
    64–5, *65*
  belts, buckles and clasps 66–7, *67*
  bodice fasteners 54–8, *54–7*
  brooches 63–4, *64*
  buttons 52, 67, *67*
  headdresses and hair ornaments
    58–60, *58–9*
  necklaces and chains 60–63, *60–63*
  rings 65–6
chains: Central Europe *53, 55,* 57–8,
  57
  Eastern Europe 124–8, *124–9, 132*
  France 74–7, *76*
  Italy 83, 89–92, *92*
  Nordic region 34
Chile 102
China 98, 108
choker necklaces 34, 45, *45,* 60
Cieszyn 54, *54*
clasps: Central Europe *10,* 54

Eastern Europe *16,* 119–24,
  120–23, 130
  France 74, *75*
  Netherlands 45–6, *46*
  Nordic region 27–8, *29*
coins 65
Cole, Henry 14–17, 19
collar links 38–9
combs 108, *108, 111*
coral 11, 60–63, 65, *65, 82, 91,* 124
Cordoba 98, *111*
Croatia: brooches 64
  buttons 133
  clasps 124
  necklaces 128
  watch chains *127*
crosses: Eastern Europe 131, *131*
  France *69–74, 70–73, 79*
  Italy 81, 85–7, *87–8*
  Netherlands 45
  Spain and Portugal 102–4, *103–4*
  Nordic region 34–7, *34, 36*
crowns, bridal 32–4, *33*
crucifixes 34, 88, 102–4, *104–5*
cuff links 39
Cyprus: chains 124, 126, *129*
  clasps 120, *120, 122*
  hair pins 114

Dachery, P-A. *74*
Dahlberg, Gabriel *36*
Dalmatia *13*
  belts and clasps 119, 124
  buttons 133, *133*
  crosses 70
  earrings 119
  hair pin 116
  watch chains *127*
deer's teeth *9*
Denmark: buttons 39
  headdress 34
diadems *33,* 34, 114, *114,* 116
diamond 77,
doublets 83
dowry jewellery 11–12, 92
  see also marriage jewellery

earrings 14
  Central Europe 58–9
  Eastern Europe *11,* 116–19, *116–19*
  France 69–70, *69*
  Italy 81, *84–6,* 84–5
  Netherlands 43, *43*
  Spain and Portugal 98–102, *98–102*
Eastern Europe 112–33
  belts and clasps 119–24, *120–23*
  bracelets 131–3
  buttons 133, *133*
  chains 124–8, *124–9, 132*
  earrings 116–19, *116–19*
  headdresses 114, *114*
  religious pendants and amulets
    128–31, *130–32*
enamel: Bressan 70, 78–9, *79*
  Cyprus 124
  Eastern Europe *122,* 124
  North Africa 97
England 14–19

Epirus 11
  chains 129
  clasps 14, *15*
Estonia 26–7, *126*
evil eye 85, 88, *90*, 107
Extremadura 97

filigree 11
  Central Europe *10*, 54, *55*, *57*, *58*,
    60, *60*, 63–7, 67
  Eastern Europe *117*, *119–23*,
    120–24, *127*, 131, *132–3*
  France *70–71*, 79
  Italy *83–6*, *88–91*, 92–3, *93–5*, 95
  Netherlands *43*, 45, 46, *46*, *48–9*, 49
  Nordic region 21, *29*, *31*, *33*, 34, 36,
    37, 39, *39*
  Spain and Portugal 98, *98*, *100*,
    102–4, *103–7*, 111, *111*
Finland: ring brooches 26, *27*
Flinkenberg, A.R. *38*
Föhr *51*, 55
France 68–79
  belt hooks 78, *78*
  Bressan enamels 70, 78–9, *79*
  brooches 77–8, *77*
  clasps 74, *75*
  crosses and religious pendants
    69–74, *70–73*, 79
  dowry jewellery 11
  earrings 69–70, *69*
  necklaces 17, *17*, 74–7, *76*
  silversmiths 9–11
Frisia 41
Fritz, Johann Friedrich *51*

Galicia *100*
garnets 11, *11*, *44*, 45, *53*, *60*, 63, *64*,
  82, 86, 88, 99
Germany 51, 52
  amulets *65*
  belts *18*, 67
  bodice fasteners 54, *55*, 57–8, *57*
  brooches 63, *64*
  buckles 67
  buttons 67, *67*
  filigree *10*, 11
  necklaces *18*, *19*, *62*, 63
  rings *9*, 65–6, *66*
  silversmiths 9
Goldsmiths' Company of London 22
Greece *7*, 113
  amulets *130*
  chains 128, *128–9*
  clasps *15*, *120*, *130*
  earrings 116
  filigree 124
Grinderud, Tor *24*
Gubrandsdal *39*
Guibray 11

hair ornaments 14
  Central Europe 58, *58–9*
  Eastern Europe 114
  Italy 81, *90*, 93–5, *94–5*
  Netherlands 42–3, *42–5*
  Spain and Portugal 107–8, *108–11*
Hamburg 52, 63, 67, *67*

Hammer, Marius 21
Hanius, M. *52*
headdresses 9
  Central Europe 58–60
  Eastern Europe 114, *114*
  Italy *92–3*, 92–3
  Netherlands 42–3, *42–5*
  Nordic region 32–4, *32–3*
Hetzeldorfer, M. *52*
Holmberg, E. *38*
Holy Land 124
Hudson's Bay Company 26
Hungary 51, 52, *53*, 57, 60, 67

Iceland 21
  belts 30, *31*
  bodice fasteners 27, *28*
  buttons 38, 39, *39*
  headdresses 34
  silversmiths 11
India 120
Islam 128, 133
Italy 80–95
  amulets and religious pendants 83,
    85, *86–9*, *88–90*
  belts 81–2, *82*
  crosses 81, 85–6, *86–8*, 89
  dowry jewellery 11
  earrings 81, 84–5, *84–6*
  hair pins and head ornaments 81,
    90, 92–3, *92–5*
  necklaces and chains 83, 89, *91–2*,
    95
  rings 81
  rosaries 81

Jamieson, C. *26*
jet 52–4
Jonge, J.F. de *48*

Karagouna people *7*, 126
Karelia *27*

Lapland: belts 30–32
  bodice fasteners 28, *30*
  buttons 38–9
  rings 38
Latin America 14, 102
Latvia: ring brooches 26–7, *27*
Léon 97, *100*, *104*
Lombardy *83*, 93
Lutheranism 34

Macedonia *117*, *120*
Maghreb 14, 97, 99
Malta 81, *95*
Marche *86*, *90*
marriage jewellery 11–12
  Central Europe 65–6
  Eastern Europe 114, *114*, 119–20,
    133
  France 74–7
  Italy 81–2, *82*, 93
  Netherlands 41
  Nordic region *21*, 32–4, *32–3*, 37, *37*
  Spain 104–7
men's accessories 12, *13*
Mexico 102, 108

Millais, John Everett *19*
Millberg, A.G. *24*
Minoret, J-A. *78*
Mongols 113, 114
Moors 97, 98, 107
Morocco 97–8, 99, 107
mother-of-pearl 65, *122*, 124
mourning jewellery 45, *45*
Murcia *111*

Naples: amulets 88, *89*
  buttons 95
  earrings *84–5*
  hair pin *94–5*
  necklaces *91*
necklaces: Central Europe *18*, *19*,
  60–63, *60–63*
  France *17*, 74–7, *76*
  Italy 83, 89, *91–2*, 95
  Netherlands 45, *45*
  Nordic region 34–8, *36–7*
  Spain 97, 104–7, *107*
Netherlands 14, 40–49
  buttons 46–9, *46–9*
  clasps and buckles 45–6, *46*, 74
  headdresses and hair ornaments
    42–3, *42–5*
  necklaces and pendants 45, *45*
  silversmiths 9
niello *16*, *26*, *120*, *126*, 129, 131
Nordic region 21–39
  belts 30–32, *33*
  bodice fasteners 27–8, *28–30*
  buttons 38–9, *38–9*
  headdresses 32–4, *32–3*
  necklaces and pendants 34–8, *36–7*
  ring brooches 22–7, *22–7*
  rings 38, *38*
Normandy 11, 69, 71, 73, *73*, 74, 75,
  76, 77
North Africa 14, 97–8
North America 15, 78
Norway 11, 14
  belts 30, *31*, 32
  bodice fasteners 27–8, *28–9*
  bridal jewellery *21*
  buttons 39, *39*
  headdresses 32–4, *32–3*
  pendants 37–8, *37*
  ring brooches 22, *22–5*, 27
  rings 38, *38*
  silversmiths 21–2

oorijzer 42–3, *42*, 45
Oporto *105*
Orthodox Church 14, 124, 128
Ottoman Empire 113, 114, 119, 120,
  133

Papal States *86*, *90*
Paris 69
paste *9*, *11*, 14, *25*, 28, *29*, 34, *36*, 38,
  45, 52, 57, 58, *58*, 63, *63*, 64, *66*,
  73, *73*, 77, 83, 114
pearls *9*, 11, *11*, *18*, *53*, 83, *84*, 85, 88,
  91, *104*, *112*, 114, 116, *116*
pendants: Central Europe *52*, 65, *65*
  Eastern Europe 128–31, *131*

France *69–74*, *70–73*, *79*
Italy 83, *84–6*, *86*, *88–90*, 89–92
Nordic region *8*, 34–8, *36–7*
Spain and Portugal 104, *105*
Persia 120
Peter the Great, Tsar 113
Pettersson, J.E. *38*
Philippines 102, 108
Piedmont 95
Poissant, V. *70*
Poitou 74, *78*
Poland 51
  belts 67
  bodice fasteners 54, 57
  brooches 63–4
  necklaces 60, 63
Portaels, Jean *81*
Portugal 97–111
  earrings 98–102, *101*
  rosaries, religious pendants and
    amulets 104–7, *105–7*
Pre-Raphaelites 19
Protestantism 34, 41, 46–9, 51, 58
Provence 71, 77

religious jewellery 14
  Central Europe 64–5, *65*
  Eastern Europe 128–31, *130–32*
  France *69–74*, *70–73*
  Italy 83, 86–9, *88–90*
  Nordic region *8*, 34–7, *36*
  Spain and Portugal 104–7, *105*
ring brooches *see* brooches
rings 9
  Central Europe *9*, 65–6
  Italy 81
  Netherlands 41
  Nordic region 38, *38*
rock crystal 11, 65, 71, *73*
Romagna 88, *89*
Romania *120*, 128
rosaries 64–5, 81, 86, 89, 102, 104–7
rubies *11*, *84*
Russia 113, *113*, 114
  buttons 113, 133
  chains 124–6, *124–5*, *132*
  earrings *11*, 116, *116*
  headdresses 114
  religious pendants 131, *131–2*

Salamanca 98, 99, 102, *102–4*, *107*,
  111, *111*
Sami people 28, *30*, 32
Santiago de Compostela *98*, 104
Saphrampolis 124
sapphires *84*
Saragossa *98*, 104
Sarakatsani people 126
Sardinia 83, *84*, 86, 88, 92, *92*, 95, *95*
Savoy 69, 71–3, 86
Saxons 51, *52*, 67
Schoonhoven 9
Schwäbisch Gmünd 9, 11, 52–4, 64,
  65, 66, *66*, 67
Scotland 22–6, *26*, 37
Serbia 116
Seville 98
Sicily 82, *82*, 85, 95

Index

silversmiths 9–11
Skåne 28, *29*, 34, *34*, *36*, 38, *38*
Slavs 113, 116, 133
Slovakia 57, 63–4, 67
Slovenia 67
South America 97, 99–102
South Kensington Museum 14–19, 73
southeast Asia 14, 97
Spain 97–111
   buttons 111, *111*
   crosses 102–4, *103–4*
   earrings 98–102, *98–100*, *102*
   hair pins 107–8, *108*
   necklaces *97*
   rosaries, religious pendants and
   amulets 104–7, *105–7*
Sri Lanka 14
Strøm, Fredrik *22*
Sweden: belts 30
   bodice fasteners 27, 28, *28–9*
   bridal jewellery 34, *34*
   buttons 38–9, *38*
   necklaces and pendants *8*, 34–8,
    34–6
   ring brooches 22, *24–5*
   rings 38, *38*
   silversmiths 9
Switzerland 14, 51, 81
   bodice fasteners 57–8, *57*
   brooches 63, 64
   hair ornaments 58, *58–9*
   necklaces and chains 34, 60–63, *60*
   religious jewellery 65, *65*

tau crosses 34–7, *34*, *36*
teeth, deer's *9*
Telemark 22, *24*, *25*, 27–8, *29*
Thessaly *7*, *128*
Thornhill, W.H. *16*, 32
Thrace 119, 133
Ticino 81
Tidemand, Adolph *32*
toggle buttons 83, *95*, 111, *111*, *133*
Tostrup, Jacob 21
Transylvania 12, 51, *52*
   belts *14*, 67
   pendants *52*
Turin 86
Tuscany *84*, 88
turquoise *14*, *64*, *119*

United States of America 17

Valencia 99, *103*, 108, *108*, *111*
Vendée 77, *77*
Venice 84, *84–5*, 89, 133
verre eglomisé 66
Vierland 63, *64*
Vogel, Ludwig *58*
Volendam 42

Wahlberg, J. *29*
waist clasps 14
Walcheren *41*
Wallengren, P.M. *25*, *29*
wedding jewellery *see* marriage jewellery
Woodlands Indians 14, *15*, 26
Württemberg 57–8

Ydot, Paul *79*
Ystad *29*

Zamora 99
Zeeland 41, *41*, *42*, 43